You Can Feel Good Again

Good News About Depression

Richard Carlson, Ph.D.

Thorsons

An Imprint of HarperCollinsPublishers

Thorsons
An Imprint of HarperCollins*Publishers*
77—85 Fulham Palace Road,
Hammersmith, London W6 8JB

Published by Thorsons 1993
1 3 5 7 9 10 8 6 4 2

A catalogue record for this book
is available from the British Library

ISBN 0 7225 2867 1

Phototypeset by Harper Phototypesetters Limited,
Northampton, England
Printed in Great Britain by
HarperCollinsManufacturing Glasgow

You Can Feel Good Again

Richard Carlson has a PhD in psychology. He is the author and editor of several popular books exploring the fields of psychology and happiness. Dr Carlson is a frequent lecturer and maintains a private practice in stress management and happiness training in California. He is happily married and has two wonderful children.

Contents

For a list of books, tapes, and practitioners
teaching healthy psychological functioning,
send a written request along with a stamped,
self-addressed envelope to:

Happiness Training
P.O. Box 1196
Orinda, CA 94563
USA

Introduction

I respectfully ask that you try to forget everything you have ever been told about unhappiness, pessimism and depression — where these feelings come from, how serious they are, and how difficult they are to overcome. Try to forget about all the attempts you have made that have failed and all the approaches that promised results but did not deliver. Even though I am going to explain how you can begin to feel better *today*, I don't ask you to believe me with blind faith. Instead, I ask that you use your own common sense when evaluating what you are about to read. By the time you finish this book I believe you will not only feel better, but also understand exactly why most approaches failed you before.

The way to get the most out of this book is to approach it with an open mind. See whether it makes sense to you and if it sounds like something that you already know intuitively. Some of what I propose will be quite different from what you have been exposed to before. Don't let this be an obstacle to getting the help you deserve. Keep in mind that if what you have already learned was the answer you were looking for, you wouldn't be reading this book today. You would be out enjoying your life.

The information given here is different because it represents a *new understanding* in the field of mental health. It doesn't build on other approaches you may already be familiar with. If you can digest and 'take to heart' the information in this book, you will feel better right away. There is very little effort involved; all you have to do is understand what you read on an intuitive level and make a gentle effort to put your understanding into practice. As you will see, I don't offer any fancy techniques or any sophisticated psychological theories to sift through. What I offer you is a simple yet profound common-sense-based understanding of mental health and happiness that really works, and that can be implemented immediately. I have seen people who have been unhappy or depressed for as many as 30 years walk away from my office feeling better than they can ever remember. And what's more, the good feeling you will learn to tap into sticks with you.

I am a stress-management consultant who teaches people some very simple facts about their own internal functioning — what makes them tick and what makes them fall apart. The principles that I teach are generic, meaning they apply to everyone. I receive referrals from therapists around the country who have seen their clients rid themselves of depression as a result of what I teach. As people learn about the habitual processes that contribute to their own misery, and the ways that they use their own minds to sabotage their lives, they quickly discover a natural and relatively effortless way to escape the grips of unhappiness and lifelong pessimism.

My approach is based on a set of principles known as the Psychology of Mind.* It is being used by growing

* The Psychology of Mind was founded by Mr Syd Banks, Dr Roger Mills and Dr George Pransky. The principles in this book are extrapolated from the three principles of the Psychology of Mind but are not the actual principles. Readers can learn more about Psychology of Mind by sending a stamped addressed envelope to: Happiness Training, P.O. Box 1196, Orinda, CA 94563, USA.

numbers of therapists, consultants and educators, with spectacular results! The methods you will learn have been extrapolated from these principles in a way that is geared towards freeing you from unhappiness.

Many professionals now teaching this approach have come to believe that a majority of the more 'conventional' therapeutic approaches available today to treat unhappiness can actually make matters worse instead of better. This is not to say that there aren't excellent, well-qualified therapists practising traditional therapy — there most certainly are. What you may discover, however, is that many of the practices that therapists currently use tend to fuel an already depressed state. Clients are directed to 'get in touch' with their most negative feelings and analyse their pasts in order to transcend their present situations. They are asked to study, if not relive, their childhood as well as their more recent past so that they can better understand the psychological damage that was inflicted on them.

One of the consistent problems I have seen in working with clients who have 'given up' on traditional therapy is that each time a new trauma is uncovered, the client is in effect starting over again. There are always new sessions designed to get to the bottom of each additional 'issue' and to explore the negative feelings that go along with recounting them. Each specific issue entails more negative feelings to explore. Many therapists insist that unless people deal head-on with their negative experiences and unconscious drives, they will be miserable forever. You must keep in mind, when deciding whether traditional therapy makes sense to you, that the therapists who tell you this are almost always paid by the hour!

In defence of therapists, I don't think I've ever met one who would intentionally keep a client longer than they felt was absolutely necessary. Nevertheless, there is a certain conflict of interest to be very cautious of: if you get better, the therapist loses you as a client! If you have been in therapy for an extended period of time and are still unhappy, you may want to reconsider your treatment. Is more of the same *really* going to help? Is going deeper into your pain and suffering *really* going to help you experience joy? Is getting in touch with more negativity *really* going to make you feel less negative? I doubt it. History shows us that this route often doesn't work.

Does this mean that therapy is useless? No. I would say, however, that success in therapy depends far more on the mental health and happiness of the therapist than it does on reliving past traumas and pain. A skilled therapist who is also a happy, vibrant person will most certainly be able to pass along at least some of her happiness almost regardless of the specific approach she uses.

One of the most striking observations that many people make when attending a Psychology of Mind seminar or when they have a private session with a consultant, is that the people who teach Psychology of Mind are very happy people themselves. I have come to believe that unless a person is happy himself, it's very difficult, if not impossible, to teach someone else to be happy. How can an unhappy person, who is caught up in personal problems, teach an already unhappy person to feel joy? I feel grateful to be able to say that I am, indeed, a happy person, and I hope the feeling I bring to life will touch you as you read this book.

Who is this Book For?

Carl Jung once said, 'The greatest affliction affecting mankind isn't serious mental illness — but the general uneasiness and unhappiness that is so prevalent in our society.' Jung believed, as I do, that many people experience life in a 'lifeless' manner. Many if not most people have lost touch with the mystery and magic that surrounds us. The first step towards living fully is simply feeling better.

This book was written for anyone who would like to feel better than they presently do — anyone who frequently experiences 'the blues', ongoing sadness, a pessimistic outlook, frequent unhappiness, internal misery, a lack of gratitude about the gift of life — or someone who simply wishes to *feel better*. It is an outgrowth of an earlier book, *You Can Be Happy No Matter What* (New World Library, 1992). I received hundreds of letters and phone calls from readers who appreciated the principles of happiness that I spoke about, yet wanted to hear more specifically about how to get themselves out of the 'lower states of mind' that pessimistic people find themselves in.

The approach to happiness outlined in this book can help virtually anyone improve their mental outlook and the quality of their life. It should *not*, however, be used in lieu of professional treatment if you suffer from serious depression, suicidal urges or other serious mental illness. If you experience serious depression, please seek professional guidance *before* reading this book and attempting to implement the philosophy. Your doctor or counsellor may want you to use the ideas presented here in conjunction with your therapy. I certainly hope so, but please check first.

This book was written to address Jung's assessment of the state of humankind, the general level of unhappiness that surrounds us. I will show you how to rid yourself of the negative feelings that can take over your life and replace them with the feelings of gratitude, happiness and love.

I will also show you how to access a place within yourself where 'feeling good' already exists, as well as how to detect those mental processes that take you away from this place. I have never met a person who didn't feel better after learning this simple approach. Once you learn how *you* create unhappiness in your life with your own thinking — and once you learn how to stop this pattern — you will certainly be far more hesitant to continue or return to any destructive psychological tendencies you may have.

Approach the ideas here with an open mind and a curious heart. Don't discount anything as being too simplistic until you have had an honest chance to practise what you learn and assess how you feel. If you read with your own common sense as your guide — remembering that your goal is to be happier — I believe you will be pleasantly surprised at how good you can feel. It really is true: you *can* feel good again.

1

Possibilities

Jim and Yvonne had been married for 32 mostly unhappy years when they discovered that Jim had a cancerous life-threatening tumour. Prior to discovering this information, the couple had lived together in an almost constant state of irritation. There was frequent conflict and anger, ongoing disputes and disagreement on virtually every issue surrounding their lives together. Their love for each other had been, in Jim's words, 'lost many years ago'.

A curious thing happened the moment they found out about the tumour. Both Jim and Yvonne experienced a *sudden shift* in their consciousness. The anger that had suffocated their love for so many years disappeared, their disagreements faded away and now seemed insignificant, and their love for one another resurfaced, almost magically, as though it had never left to begin with.

What happened? This couple experienced what is commonly referred to as 'a change of heart'. No one knows exactly how or when this kind of sudden shift or change will occur, but we do know that they exist and that they are possible.

A sudden shift in consciousness can occur in any area of human life that has to do with how we feel, whether it be relationships, feeling anxious, feeling down, or any other immobilizing emotion. Consider an eight-year-old child who goes to bed every night frightened by the thought of an imagined monster behind the wardrobe door. Suddenly, one day, out of nowhere, she realizes that the monster isn't real, that it exists only in her own mind. Interesting questions include: Why did the child have this realization on this particular day? What was it that made her realize the monster wasn't real? The answers to these questions are surprisingly vague. We don't know for sure, except to say that a new level of understanding surfaced within the consciousness of the child.

Another example of a sudden shift is the person who swears that he is going to stop smoking. Week after week, year after year, he promises he's going to do it. You, as a friend, have heard the same story many times. Then, one day, for no apparent reason, your friend tells you the very same thing, only this time you know that he means it. Something is different. Something has changed. You can't quite put your finger on it, but you know he will never smoke again. And indeed, he never does.

While the particulars of each sudden shift are unique, there are common denominators that seem to exist in all cases. First, the 'shift' itself doesn't necessarily build on what we already know, but instead is seen *suddenly,* as if out of nowhere. In other words, the amount of information we have on the subject isn't the critical factor. For example, I was working with a client, George, who had spent his entire life feeling prejudice about people of a specific race. He had a sudden shift in his perspective and realized (in his words), 'What a fool I have been.' What made this particular example so intriguing to me was that the two of us had *never* spoken about his prejudice. I never even knew he had this problem. His realization came about as he was discussing how his own thinking sometimes got in the way of his relationship with his wife. The shift that occurred in his consciousness was achieved without obtaining additional information about 'the problem'. He had intellectually known for years that all prejudice stems from ignorance, yet he still felt prejudice, until that moment. Something shifted within him while he was thinking about something else.

I had a sudden shift of my own that is equally difficult to explain. I had spent my entire life frightened to death of public speaking. The very thought of speaking to a group made me sweat, and in two instances I actually fainted! Then, one day while eating lunch with some friends at a conference I was attending, I realized there was nothing to fear. I can't explain exactly why or how I had this insight, only that it happened. To this day, I am very comfortable speaking to groups of any size and do so quite frequently.

Second, sudden shifts are accompanied by a feeling of inspiration, sometimes described as 'a light feeling', or 'a nice feeling'. Yvonne and Jim each described their sudden shift as a 'feeling of incredible relief', as though a huge emotional burden had been lifted. Many clients have reported to me similar feelings of being 'uplifted' in some powerful way as they experienced an insight that changed the way they looked at life. This feeling is often described as a sense of self-confidence. Later, I will discuss this in a context of your healthy psychological functioning.

Finally, sudden shifts are permanent in nature. When a shift occurs, there doesn't seem to be any turning back, at least not all the way. For example, it's hard for me to imagine being frightened by the act of speaking to a group. I can, however, have empathy for those who do, because I remember what it feels like. The idea of Yvonne and Jim hating each other, as they did for so long, seems ridiculous. And my client George chuckles at the thought of disliking someone because of the colour of his skin. This the nature of insight — it happens, and from that moment forward life looks different.

An interesting and important point about sudden shifts is this: *there is no relationship between the 'feeling better' aspect of sudden shifts and the external appearance of life getting better.* So, for example, a person who experiences a sudden shift in the way she feels about her finances didn't do so because she had just inherited a large estate or won the football pools. She experienced the shift because she looked at the same set of facts in a new way. Whatever it was that she saw, it affected her enough that money will no longer be a source of inner conflict in her life.

Certainly Yvonne and Jim were no better off. To the contrary, Jim was given a terminal diagnosis. Yet both he and Yvonne felt more love for each other than ever before.

Likewise, the child who had the realization about the imagined monster in her wardrobe wasn't any better off. The monster was never there to begin with! This is the nature of sudden shifts. They occur through a shift in understanding — not through a change in circumstance.

This is a book about possibilities. Be open to the possibility that this book will help you have your own sudden shift. If you do, your experience of life will change before your eyes. You will feel better, more joyful, more relaxed, and more secure. Absolutely nothing needs to change in your life in order for you to feel better. You simply need to see something about the nature of your own thinking that you didn't see before. Your sudden shift can happen instantly and it can be profound.

Commitment

As you will see throughout this book, happiness is a moment-to-moment choice that each of us makes. In order to be happy, you must first *decide* to be happy. You must make a commitment to happiness.

It's important to know that commitment to learning the art of happiness is not exactly what it seems to be at first glance. Most people make the mistake of confusing commitment to happiness with the decision to make their life better in some way. Although these two ideas seem related, they are not necessarily so. As you have probably noticed, you can change everything in your life without affecting your level of happiness one single bit. You can earn more money, get yourself out of trouble, meet new friends, get a new job, solve a problem, get a degree, get married, or acquire something you have always wanted, yet still feel unsatisfied. The reason for this is that happiness exists independently of your circumstances; it's a feeling that you can learn to live in.

The way to get the most out of this book is to approach it with the understanding that it's possible to learn to be happy *without changing anything in your life – except your relationship to your own thinking*. The American philosopher Emerson once said, 'The ancestor to every action is a thought.' Everything in your life is a function of the way you relate to your thinking. As you think, so shall you be.

Commitment is a powerful tool for change. It takes pressure off you by removing the uncertainty that often accompanies a lack of commitment. Marriage, for example, is a commitment. When a couple gets married there is a reasonable belief that, regardless of what might happen, the commitment will carry the couple through. Prior to marriage, people often feel insecure about losing their partner. The commitment relieves their anxiety and gives them the freedom to 'let go' of their concerns; it fosters hope.

Without commitment, success in any venture is difficult. Whether you are dieting, studying for an exam, learning to play tennis, starting a project or deciding to be happy, commitment is an important step.

When you make a commitment to happiness you are in effect saying: *'There is so much in life that I can't control – the world, other people and their choices and reactions, accidents, imperfections, suffering, hardships. Yet this is my life and regardless of what happens, I'm going to be happy.'*

Whenever you attach conditions to your happiness you won't experience it. The same mental process that attaches your happiness to a specific outcome will only repeat that pattern once that outcome is obtained. A person who believes that 'having children' will make her happy will then create new conditions to be met once the children arrive. She may then believe that she will be happy when the infant stage is over, or the terrible two's, or when she has enough money to meet her growing family's needs. Your commitment to happiness itself allows you to let go of all your preconditions. Instead of having conditions, you say to yourself: 'No matter how difficult it seems, I'm going to practice the mental processes that will lead me to happiness.'

Being happy isn't always easy. In fact, it can be one of the great challenges in life. True maturity means taking responsibility for our own happiness — right now. It means choosing to concentrate on what we have instead of what we lack.

Commitment is the first step in allowing you to regain the positive feelings that you are looking for. Most of us believe that by solving our problems, or improving our relationships, we will find contentment, but this means that our happiness must be postponed until some future date when those conditions are met. Commitment is a step towards bringing that future to the present.

Happiness is the result of a decision to be happy. You may believe that you will one day arrive at a place called happiness, that one day everything will fall into place and you will be able to say: 'Great, here I am. I've made it to happiness land.' Obviously, this isn't going to happen. Regardless of how good your life gets and how many of your dreams come true, you will still have to make the decision to be happy. You will still have to make the commitment. There is no way *to* happiness. Happiness *is* the way!

The information in this book will act as a navigational tool that will guide you towards happiness. Remember that your goal is to be happy. Make the commitment and use the tools in this book to take you there. So let's get started!

2

Your Thoughts and the Way You Feel

We are all constantly thinking — and it's a good thing that we do! Without the ability to think, our lives would seem to have little significance. It's important to realize that you are constantly thinking. Don't be fooled into believing that you are already aware of this fact, because you probably are not. Think, for a moment, about your breathing. Until the moment I brought it to your attention, you had most certainly lost sight of the fact that you were doing it. Breathing is so natural and automatic that unless you are out of breath you simply forget that you're doing it.

Thinking works the same way. Because you're always doing it, it's easy to forget that it's happening, and it becomes invisible to you. Unlike breathing, however, forgetting that you are thinking, even for a moment, can cause some serious problems in your life, including unhappiness, even depression. The reason is that your thinking will always come back to you as a feeling. Let me explain: the way you feel right now is the result of your thoughts at this very moment. In a broader sense, the way you feel is always determined by the thoughts you are thinking. Suppose you have the thought as you are reading this material. 'This is far too simplistic — my problems are far more serious than Dr Carlson could possibly imagine.' The result of this thought would be that you would be feeling sceptical and pessimistic right now. This is not a coincidence. Before you had these thoughts, you weren't feeling pessimistic. Your thoughts created your sceptical feeling, the words I have written did not. If the words themselves created feelings, then everyone who read them would feel the same way, which of course they don't. The relationship between your thinking and how you are feeling is formed so fast (in a tiny fraction of a second) that almost no one realizes it's occurring. Yet this cause-and-effect relationship between thoughts and feelings is one of the most powerful phenomena you will ever experience as a human being.

Now suppose that as you were reading the morning paper, you came across an article about a little girl who was rescued from a burning building. As you read the story you had the thought, 'What a relief.' As soon as you had this inspiring thought you felt an uplifting of your spirits. Again, your emotion was created by your thoughts about the event — not the event itself. If you had thought differently, you would have felt differently. For example, if you had the thought, 'It's about time they included a happy story. The papers are always filled with bad news,' you wouldn't have felt uplifted but pessimistic. The feelings that accompany the thoughts you are having happen in an instant. This psychological dynamic is true all the time — there are no exceptions. Whenever you have a thought, and believe that thought to be true, you will feel a corresponding emotional response to that thought. *Your thoughts always create your emotions.* Understanding the significance of this fact is the first step in escaping from unhappiness and depression.

Negative and pessimistic thoughts, regardless of their specific content, are the root cause of all of your negative and self-defeating emotions. In fact, it's neurologically impossible for you to feel anything without first having a thought — you simply wouldn't have a reference point. Try feeling guilty without first thinking guilty thoughts. Try feeling angry without thinking about something that makes you angry. You can't do it. In order to experience an event, you must process that event in your mind thereby interpreting it and giving it meaning and significance. This understanding has enormous implications. It suggests that if you feel unhappy, it's not your life, your circumstances, your genes, or your true nature that is creating your unhappiness — it's your thinking. Unhappiness doesn't, and can't, exist on its own. Unhappiness is the feeling that accompanies your negative thinking about your life. In the absence of that thinking, the unhappiness can't exist. There is nothing to hold your negative feelings in place other than your thinking.

I am not saying that there are never physiological components that compound an unhappy or depressed state, or that make a person predisposed to unhappiness or depression. I am saying, however, that without thought there is no fuel to throw on the fire, there is nothing to foster the predisposition or physiological components into a reality.

It's interesting to note that there have always been people who would seem to have every reason to be depressed — circumstances that depress some of us just hearing about them: helpless poverty, unbelievable hardships, cruel treatment by others. But some people simply don't experience unhappiness regardless of how serious their circumstances appear to be. They make the best out of the situation they are in. There are other people who apparently have every reason to feel happiness and contentment, people who are often tormented by depression. Rather than appreciating what they have, they focus on what they would rather have.

Thinking Turns Events into Problems

Let's suppose that two of your friends are getting divorced. You had always assumed that if anyone could make it, this couple could. On Wednesday, the couple started divorce proceedings, and a week later your friend called you to tell you the news. 'Oh no,' you say and instantly begin to feel bad. Interesting, isn't it? The event has already taken place, it's long over. But now, as you think about the event, you start to feel bad. Clearly the event itself didn't make you feel bad. It happened seven days ago and you didn't even know about it. Your thoughts about the event are the guilty party, responsible for the way you feel. The event was certainly 'real' but it meant nothing to you — it was neutral — until you were able to bring it to life through your thinking. Interestingly enough, had your thinking interpreted the divorce differently, you would have felt differently. You may just as easily have thought to yourself, 'Oh well, I suppose only they can know what is best for them.' This thought may have left you with a feeling of compassion and understanding.

Think of a more mundane example — snow. For some people snow means snowballs, sledges, skiing, and snowmen. For these people, snow is cause for great celebration! For others, however, snow means dead batteries, a slushy mess, cold weather, and so on. In short, the snow is cause for a lot of complaining. Take note, however, that the snow itself doesn't care how you think about it. The snow is neutral. It just exists and goes on being snow. It doesn't cause the positive *or* the negative reactions and feelings you may have. Only your thinking can do that for you. I hope this illustrates how you use your thinking to create emotional responses which give you an experience of life. Your thinking, not the events themselves, cause your emotional responses.

Your Thoughts Aren't Real

If you could understand that your thoughts aren't real you could stop reading right now, because you would feel a tremendous sense of relief and you would have realized how to create happiness in your life — forever. And even though it *is* going to take some explanation on my part, the statement is true. Think about it: your thoughts aren't real. They *are* real thoughts, but they're not the same thing as concrete 'reality'.

When you think, you are using your imagination to create an image or picture in your mind of an event rather than the real thing. If you are driving home from a football match, reviewing the game in your mind, you are merely imagining what the game was like. The game is no longer real, it's now only in your mind, in your memory. It was real once, but not any longer. Similarly, if you are thinking about how bad your marriage is, you are considering it in your mind. *It's all in your imagination.* You are literally 'making up' your relationship. The thoughts you are having about your relationship are just thoughts. This is why the old saying, 'Things aren't as bad as they seem' is almost always true. The reason things 'seem so bad' is because your mind is able to re-create past events, and preview upcoming events, almost as though they were happening right in front of you, at that moment — even though they're not. To make matters worse, your mind can add additional drama to any event, thereby making that event seem even worse than it really is, or was, or will be. Even more important, your mind can review the imagined event dozens of times in a matter of seconds! This is very important to understand, because while an actual event such as an argument with a friend can last a minute or two, your mind can recreate that very event, magnify it, and make it last three hours — or an entire lifetime. But that argument is no more real *now* than an argument you had with your father ten years ago. The point is that *now*, when your life is really happening, that remembered argument is just a thought, an event being created within your own mind.

If you can begin to see that your thoughts are not the real thing — they're just thoughts, and as thoughts they can't hurt you — your entire life will begin to change today. I have witnessed many times this very same realization transform someone from a life of fear and depression into a life of happiness.

What would you say to a nine-year-old child who was convinced that a nasty witch was behind her door? Would you have her come to your home weekly to describe the witch to you in great detail? Would you have her think about it constantly? No, you would probably tell her that the witch wasn't real, that it was only an imagined witch. With your help, eventually the child will understand that the witch was only real in her mind. Once this happens, she will no longer be frightened.

Taking this same understanding one step further, what would you say to the same child if she said to you, 'My life is a failure, no one likes me, I never have any fun, I don't want to live.' Wouldn't you also try to teach her that the thoughts she was having about herself were just thoughts? I hope so. There is nothing holding those ideas in place other than her own thinking, her own internal dialogue. If the nine-year-old were able to see what you were trying to teach her, if she were able to establish a different type of relationship with her thinking, wouldn't she be better off than if she believed that her thoughts were real? She certainly would be. Wouldn't it be nice if she could relate to all of her thoughts in the same way?

Understanding That You Are the Thinker

You are the thinker of your own thoughts. Sounds obvious enough, but read on and I believe you will discover that, until now, you may have lost sight of this important fact.

Thinking is something that you are doing, moment by moment, to create your experience of life. But because your own thinking is so close to you, it's easy to forget that *you* are the one using your own thoughts against yourself. Here is an example. A gentleman came into my stress-management office and said, 'I'm mad at my boss. I don't like my job. I don't like the people that work with me. No one appreciates my work. I'm really angry.' When I began teaching him about how his own thinking creates his angry feelings he said, 'With all due respect, Dr Carlson, I'm angry almost all the time, but I almost never think angry thoughts.' Do you see where he was being fooled? Until that moment, he believed that 'thinking' meant the same thing as 'pondering'. Even though he may not have dwelled on his misery for hours at a time, he was nevertheless continually thinking negatively, a moment here and a moment there. He spent nearly all of his time thinking about the little things that irritated and annoyed him. It was almost as if the unstated goal of his life was to analyse it and to give his opinions on how various things affected him. His negative thoughts were creating his negative feelings and emotions and he didn't even know he was thinking them. He was a victim of his own thinking.

Because my client didn't even realize that he was thinking, he had no way of knowing that his feelings were coming from his thinking. He thought his feelings came from his job and from the people he worked with. Until we spoke, my client had never realized that he was the thinker of his own thoughts — and that those thoughts were the source of his unhappiness. He believed that his thoughts were being generated by what was going on around him, rather than from within him. He didn't realize at a deep enough level that he is the author, the producer, and the creator of his own thinking, that his thinking is something he is doing all day long, and that his doing it is the cause of most of his emotional suffering. Once he realized this he had a very inspiring insight that I have since used over and over again with clients: *Being upset by your own thoughts is similar to writing yourself a nasty letter – and then being offended by that letter!* This insight came from a man who had spent most of his life depressed.

You are the manufacturer of your own thoughts. You are the one doing the thinking that is upsetting you; you are doing it to yourself. Once you understand this important point, it's silly to go on being angered, annoyed, frightened, or depressed by your own thinking. If you are thinking negative, pessimistic, sceptical, or angry thoughts and not realizing it, it's understandable and predictable that you will be depressed. And this will happen each time you lose sight of the fact that you are thinking depressing thoughts.

There is only one way out of this negative loop, and that is to understand that you are the one doing the thinking and that it is your own thinking that is creating your pain. Once you start to see that your thoughts are just thoughts, that they are not 'reality', you will be able to dismiss them and not allow them to depress you. Any thought or series of thoughts can be dismissed, but to do so effectively you must first realize that you are the one creating them. All of us will accumulate thousands of thoughts about ourselves throughout our lifetimes. Very few of us, however, remember the fact that these thoughts, regardless of their content, are just thoughts.

Just Like a Dream
One of the easiest ways to understand the harmless nature of your own thinking, and to create some

distance between yourself and your thinking, is to compare thinking with dreaming. Almost everyone has had the unfortunate experience of a nightmare. While it's happening it seems very real, but when you wake up, you realize that it was just a dream. And what is dreaming but thinking while you are asleep. That's it! While you are asleep you are still producing thoughts. Like daytime thoughts, these night-time thoughts also create an emotional response, and they can also be frightening. Just a few nights ago, one of my children woke up in the middle of the night from a bad dream. It seemed so real to her that she was actually sweating from the experience. Once she woke up, however, she felt very different. Even though she is only three years old, she realized that her dream wasn't real, that it was just her thinking.

Your wakeful thinking can be looked at with the same perspective and clarity. It seems real, but it's still just thought. And each time you forget that it's just thought, it will seem every bit as real as a nightmare. You can frighten or depress yourself with your own thinking in a matter of seconds if you don't realize that you are doing it. You can be sitting in your living-room relaxing and reading a book when a thought crosses your mind: 'I've been depressed for so long,' or 'My marriage is no good.' Can you see how seductive and tricky it can be? If you understand thought in the way that I have been discussing, you can dismiss those thoughts and others like them — you can let them go. Or, if you choose, you can follow the thoughts, remaining aware of what you are doing to yourself. As long as you know that you are in charge, that you are the one doing the thinking, you are protected. Again, it's no different than dreaming.

A person not suffering from depression will have thoughts just like yours, but with one major difference.

When he has them, he will say to himself, 'Here I go again,' or something to that effect. Sooner or later, he'll remember that *he* is the thought-producing machine — that he is doing it to himself. As soon as he has this realization, his mind will slow down and begin to clear and he will sigh with relief. He will begin to feel better and will go on with his day.

An unhappy or depressed person, on the other hand, not seeing her thoughts with proper perspective, may follow the train of thought, believe it to be real, and submit herself to ongoing pain. Even if she doesn't follow this particular train of thought, she will eventually follow some negative thought pattern which will lower her spirits. Without the understanding of how her thinking is creating her negative experience, there is little she can do to prevent her negative thoughts from spiralling downward towards depression. After all, she believes that her thoughts are real.

The solution is to see your own thoughts as thoughts, not as reality. Create some distance from them. Just like your dreams, your thoughts are coming from within your own consciousness. Your thoughts are not real, and they can't harm you, just as your nightmares are harmless. As you create some distance and perspective from your thinking you will be freed from their effects.

Certainly, everyone has his share of negative and self-defeating thoughts. The question to ask yourself is, 'How seriously do I really have to take them?' Your thoughts have no power other than what you give them.

More Than Positive Thinking

Even though positive thinking is obviously preferred to negative thinking, positive thinking alone isn't enough to pull you out of a depressed state for very long. 'Positive thinkers' are just as much at the mercy of their own thoughts as negative thinkers — that is, if they believe that thinking is something that is happening to them rather than something that they are doing. This is a subtle but key point.

Positive thoughts are still *just thoughts*. Granted, they are nicer thoughts to have — but they are still just thoughts. If you believe that you have to think positively all the time, what's going to happen when a negative thought enters your mind?

You no longer need to feel you have to make yourself think positively — you don't. If you've spent time being depressed (and if you're reading this book you probably have), you've heard hundreds of well-meaning suggestions from all sorts of people to 'think more positively'. Unfortunately, what most people who have never been depressed don't realize is that when you're depressed you can no more think positively than get in a spaceship and fly to the moon! Thinking more positively will happen naturally, without effort, as you pull yourself out of your depression. Thinking more positively is a natural extension of knowing that your thoughts can't hurt you.

The idea here is to have a different kind of relationship to your thinking — one that allows you to have thoughts of any kind without taking any of them too seriously. You can get to the point in your life where you can have a negative thought (or a series of negative thoughts) and you simply say to yourself, 'There's another one.' It will no longer be 'front page news' in your mind! As this happens you will be able to resist the urge of following every negative train of thought that enters your mind.

If you could somehow climb into the mind of a genuinely happy person, you would notice that she isn't necessarily thinking positive thoughts. Instead, she isn't thinking about much at all, other than what she is doing. Happy people understand, either instinctually or because they have been taught, that the name of the game is to enjoy life rather than to think about it. Happy people are so immersed in the process of life, absorbed in what they are doing at the moment, that they rarely stop to analyse how they are doing. If you want to verify this concept first-hand, spend some time watching a roomful of preschool children. The reason they're having such a good time is because all of their energy is directed towards enjoyment. They are immersed in whatever they happen to be doing; they aren't keeping score.

Please don't make the mistake of thinking, 'It's different with children because they aren't grown up with real problems.' To a child, problems are every bit as real as yours are to you. Children deal with very difficult, age-related, problems: parents who fight or who are separated, adults who tell them what to do, people who take away their things, and the need to be included and loved, to name just a few. The difference between adults and children and their level of happiness isn't tied to how real their problems are, but to how much attention is placed on those problems.

If you are constantly analysing or 'keeping score' of your life, you will always be able to find fault in whatever you are doing. After all, who couldn't improve? Many people even pride themselves on their ability to be on the look-out for 'what's wrong'. But if you follow thoughts like 'Life would be better if . . .' you will once again be at the mercy of your own thinking. One thought will lead to another, and then another, and so on. It's just a matter of how much negativity you can handle. Sooner or later you'll be down in the dumps. True happiness occurs when you quiet down your analytical mind, when you give it a rest.

Once you realize that your thinking is what creates your experience of life, including your depression, analysing your life will lose its appeal. You'll prefer simply to do the best that you possibly can in any given moment and pay attention to enjoying what you are doing, knowing that you can always do better.

I'm not suggesting that you shouldn't improve your life. Your life will inevitably improve as you pay more attention to living and less to how you are doing.

Thoughts Floating Down a River

Have you ever sat next to a river and watched leaves floating peacefully by? It's a very therapeutic thing to do. Each leaf is independent of the others but is still connected by the river. You can watch any leaf until it disappears out of sight. It's a very impersonal process. What I mean by 'impersonal' is that the leaves just keep on floating. They don't care if you like them or whether you'd rather they floated differently.

Your thoughts can be looked at in much the same way. Your consciousness produces an ongoing series of thoughts, one right after the other. When you focus on any particular thought, it is present and visible. Once your attention goes elsewhere, the thought disappears from your mind. Your thoughts come and go. You have surprisingly little control over the content of your own thinking unless you are actively trying to control it. Once you understand that you are the thinker of your own thoughts, and that your mind doesn't produce 'reality', it produces 'thoughts', you won't be as affected by what you think. You'll see your thinking as something that you are doing — an ability you have that brings your experience of life — rather than as the source of reality. Do you remember the old saying 'Sticks and stones may break my bones but words can never hurt me'? *Thoughts* could be substituted for *words*. Your thoughts can't hurt or depress you once you understand that they are just thoughts.

When you start to view your own thinking in this more impersonal way (in other words, looking *at* your thinking instead of being caught *in* it), you will find yourself becoming free of depression. Your thinking goes on and on, and it will continue to do so for as long as you live. But when you step back from your thinking and simply observe that you are doing it, your mind becomes free, and you open the door to experience.

Attention and Your Thinking

If your thinking determines how you are going to feel, then it's very important to understand exactly what happens when you focus your attention on your negative thinking.

Use your own common sense to answer the following question. If negative feelings are caused by negative thinking, then what possible good can it do to overanalyse the negative parts of your life? If you spend a great deal of time rehearsing potential problems, dwelling on what's wrong, and thinking and talking about problems, only two things are certain to happen. First, you will become an expert in your problems! Not an expert at solving your problems, but an expert in *describing* them. Therapists will love you! Second, you will be depressed — or at least your spirits will be low. This is true because there is a fundamental law at work here: *thoughts grow with attention!* The more attention you give to what you are thinking, the bigger that thought becomes in your mind and the more important that thought will seem. If I ask you to think of what is bothering you, you can probably provide me with an answer. If I explore your answer with you and ask you to describe it further, and speculate as to what else might go wrong, I draw you deeper into your pain. The more specific and detailed you get, the bigger the problem will become.

Now hold on a moment. A few seconds ago you were fine and you weren't even thinking about the problem. Now, with my help, you are describing a painful event as if it were really happening! But it's not happening — except in your mind. I'm the first person to admit that it is important to acknowledge a real problem. But acknowledgement and commitment to solving a problem takes a moment or two, at most. Acknowledgement is very different from dwelling on and rehearsing, or doing endless post-mortems on situations or events.

Remember, the way you feel is determined by your thoughts. So guess what: the more attention you put on *anything* that is negative, the worse you will feel. Again, I ask that you use your own wisdom and common sense to decide whether or not to believe me. Despite the popular idea that talking about and working through negative emotions is a good idea, I'm suggesting that common sense dictates otherwise. After all, people have been working through endless negative emotions for years now — and very few are much better off than when they started and many are worse off. The questions to ask yourself (and your therapist if you have one) are: when does it (the analysis) stop? When have I had enough? When do I get to feel better?

If you believe that your thoughts are real — and you are encouraged to work through the worst of them — you will end up with even more to contend with. The more you think, the bigger and more important the thoughts will seem and the more of them there will be to deal with. Because your feelings are determined by what you think, you will, by necessity, sink even lower. And, unfortunately, because you are lower, you will think even worse thoughts, which you now have to 'work through'. This endless negative spiral never takes you upwards towards the place you want to be. The spiral will end when you decide that 'enough is enough', when you 'start over' with a clean slate, with a clear mind, and when you realize that the only thing holding your depression in place is your own thinking. You must stop focusing on your depression.

Humility

As you learn this approach, and as you begin to pull out of depression, try to be easy on yourself. It takes a great deal of humility to admit that your own thinking is the cause of your suffering. Everything you have learned prior to now may have suggested otherwise. Before you realize that your thinking is causing your depression, it's easy to blame other people and the circumstances of your life for your misery. The reason for this is clear. When you feel bad, you will have the tendency to come up with a theory as to why you feel the way you do. Without knowing the actual cause, it makes sense to create a reason. As long as you can create reasons for your depression — your marital status, your job, your children, your genes, your financial situation, your future, and so forth — you can maintain the false hope that things will get better *when* . . . But you can probably see that, in actuality, this is not true. The mindset that says 'Life will be better when . . .' will create further conditions that must be met as soon as the initial conditions are satisfied. You need only to look at the countless times in your life that you received what you wanted — and happiness still eluded you — to realize that changing your circumstances isn't the answer to your problems. If it were, you'd already be happy! You wanted to graduate, you graduated. You wanted a mate, you got one. You wanted a pet, you got one. You wanted a pay-cheque, you got one. And so on. Tens of thousands of times in your life you got exactly what you wanted and yet you're still unhappy!

The solution is to have the humility to admit that all along you have been creating your own pain through your own thinking. Don't worry; almost everyone else is doing the same thing. The good news is that as soon as you see that this is true, you'll be on your way to a far better life. No matter how depressed you have been, or how long you have been depressed, the moment you can see that it's only your thinking that is holding your depression in place, you're on your way to freedom.

You Cannot Think Your Way out of Depression

In many respects, if you want to escape from depression, it's just as important to know what not to do as it is to know what to do. If you have followed what you have read thus far you will have no difficulty understanding the statement *You cannot think your way out of depression.* You could think and think for a hundred years and you would never escape from the grips of depression. The reason: when your spirits are low you will generate negative thoughts. All you will see is negativity. You already know that your thoughts determine how you feel; thus, when you think in a depressed state of mind you will only make matters worse. The famous American football coach, Vince Lombardi, once said, 'Just because you're doing something wrong, doing it more intensely isn't going to help.' No idea applies better when you are depressed. It's your thinking that lowered your spirits to begin with; doing more of the same will only make matters worse.

Fuelling the Fire

When you are depressed, the single worst thing you can do to yourself is to continue thinking — especially if you are attempting to use your thinking to pull yourself out of your depression. To do so is only 'fuelling the fire'.

Perhaps you believe, as many people do, that you can't stop thinking when you're down in the dumps. And although it can be difficult to 'stop thinking', there is an enormous difference between doing something while believing it's natural and necessary — and doing that very same thing *knowing* that it is the cause of your suffering. Once you realize that what you have been doing has been hurting you, you will find a way to stop doing it! The only reason you have tried to think your way out of depression in the past is because you knew of no other options. But you wouldn't put salt in your wound once you knew it was going to sting like crazy. Thinking while you are depressed is similar to pouring a bucketful of salt over a deep cut! As you begin to understand the dynamic between your thinking and the way you feel, you *will* be able to ease off your thinking, in much the same way that you can ease off your car's accelerator when you are stuck in the mud. Before you understand that trying harder to get out of the mud doesn't work, you are tempted to put your foot down onto the floor. After you understand the relationship between the weight of your foot and sinking deeper into the mud, however, you ease off a little bit. If you've ever been stuck in the mud in your car, you know how *tempting* it is to try to force your way out, even when you know that accelerating makes matters worse; but because you *do* know better, you are able to resist the urge. Resist the urge to think your way out of your depression and you will find yourself out of it quicker than you expected.

3

Healthy Psychological Functioning

At the core or centre of your being is something you were born with, your 'healthy psychological functioning'. Healthy functioning is not learned, it's inherent, it's your birthright, and it's always present when you are not engaged in your thinking mind or your 'personality'. Your healthy functioning is innate, it's your most natural state of mind. It's not who you think you are (your ego), it's your higher self, who you really are and who you can be. Your healthy functioning is where your wisdom lies, it is your peace of mind, your common sense, your satisfaction in life, and your feeling of wholeness.

I will refer to your healthy functioning in different ways, with words like *wisdom* and *common sense*. It doesn't matter what you call it, the words are interchangeable. Your healthy functioning is the part of you that sees beyond unhappiness; it's your source of emotional buoyancy, the part of you where true and lasting happiness exists, and the part of you that isn't disturbed when the circumstances in your life are less than perfect.

It's important to know that you were born with healthy functioning, and that it wasn't something you had to learn. The truth is, you had to learn how to have 'unhealthy functioning', you had to learn to be unhappy.

No one is born sceptical or negative. Self-doubt, self-criticism, negativity and pessimism are the result of negative thoughts that you have learned to take seriously. Your self-image and personality are a compilation of thoughts that you have about yourself, some of which may be negative. If you had never learned to take seriously negative thoughts about yourself, you wouldn't experience the feelings that go along with them today. You are the sole creator of all your negative thoughts. Your thoughts have no power to harm you other than the power you give them.

Unfortunately, if you are not taught that the thoughts you have about yourself are just thoughts, you will start to believe that they describe the way you really are. The more you believe your own thinking, the more obscured your healthy functioning becomes. Poor self-esteem is healthy functioning that has been obscured with self-doubting thoughts you have learned to take seriously. Consider this: a young child wouldn't think of asking himself, 'Am I good enough?' He would have to *learn* to ask himself such questions. Prior to learning these types of self-doubting thoughts, a child's self-image is quite healthy and intact. If you can learn to accept negative thoughts about yourself, then you can also learn to disregard and take less seriously the negative thoughts that run through your mind. And as you do, your healthy functioning will return very quickly. As the thoughts are dismissed, a more elevated feeling will return.

Your healthy functioning is an invisible but knowable force within you. It's not something that you can touch or prove, but then neither is a dream. Yet you know that dreams exist! The first steps in tapping into your healthy functioning are to trust that it does indeed exist, and then simply have the desire to access it. Remember, there are plenty of miraculous aspects of life that are invisible — thoughts, dreams, creativity, intuition, common sense, and wisdom.

The reason that healthy functioning may be so foreign to you is that when you are experiencing it, you usually don't even know it. It's such a simple, uncomplicated feeling that you don't take notice. It's not a feeling like excitement that you can easily describe. In fact, healthy functioning is easier to describe in its absence.

Healthy psychological functioning is the feeling you have when everything seems OK, when life seems simple and you have a sense of perspective. It's the feeling you get when you are able to be touched by the simple things in life — watching a child playing, the leaves falling from a tree, or the motion of a door opening. When you are engaged in healthy functioning you are able to maintain a sense of internal equilibrium irrespective of what happens to be going on around you. Healthy functioning exists independently of the external parts of your life. It's a feeling *within you* that you can learn to access.

Once you understand that healthy functioning is a part of you, you will open the door to noticing its presence in your life. Healthy functioning will become your normal mode of emotional functioning when you accept the fact of its existence. Think back to the last time you woke up on 'the right side of the bed' and you felt a sense of gratitude about your life — the last time you said to yourself, 'Life seems magical.' Even eternal pessimists have moments when the magic of life inspires them. Try to recall the last time something happened in your life that you wish hadn't happened, yet you maintained a sense of perspective, you kept your cool. Why is it that sometimes you are able to maintain your sense of perspective while at other times you feel as if you are going to lose your mind? The answer is that sometimes you are tapped into your healthy functioning and sometimes you aren't. It's interesting to note that if you have *ever* felt the feeling I am describing here — your healthy functioning — then you already *know* that it exists. It doesn't have to disappear into nothingness and then reappear by pure chance every once in a while. Like intuition, healthy functioning is an invisible force within you that you can call upon. It's a feeling that you can learn to live with. You just have to know that it's there for you and to want it to appear — and it will.

Accessing and Aligning with Strength

Wouldn't it be nice if you could learn to live in the state of mental health that I've been describing? The first step in doing so is to open your mind to the possibility. I have seen it happen to so many people that I believe it can happen for you. Know that if you have *ever* felt peaceful during a crisis, if you have ever kept your cool when others weren't able to do so, then the possibility exists for this to occur on a regular basis. This book is about helping you to align yourself with your healthy functioning, your inner feeling of peace and strength. In order to overcome unhappiness and become a happier, more joyful person, you must find something in your life that is more powerful and important than your unhappiness. Healthy functioning is more powerful and beautiful than *any* source of misery. Once you begin to recognize healthy functioning in your life, it will become the most important factor. Discovering your healthy functioning is all you need to live a genuinely happy, productive life. If a problem can't be solved while you are tapped into your healthy functioning, then it simply can't be solved.

Two simple facts can summarize much of what you need to know about people. We are all very different — and we are all very similar! When our personalities or thought systems are turned on, we are but one of literally billions of separate people with our own individual stories, ideas, complaints, and dramas. In this domain, there is separateness, friction, stress, strife, and lots of unhappiness. Everyone is actively thinking and, unfortunately, believing most of what they are thinking. There is a great deal of confusion in this domain because everyone thinks that their way is the 'right' way. But when our minds are quiet, when we are simply 'being', and are aligned with our healthy functioning, we are all, in a very important sense, the same, at least in the ways that really matter. We are peaceful and filled with peaceful feelings. We are understanding of our differences, loving, and kind to ourselves and to others. We see the bigger picture, the innocence in our differences, and we can access the beauty of life.

As I just said, you can not get rid of something as powerful as unhappiness unless you have something even more powerful to replace it with — your healthy functioning. This part of you is so much more powerful than anything you could ever 'think of'. Your healthy functioning is a place inside yourself where you can rest in your being instead of being active in your personality. It is a place of meditation — but you don't have to meditate to get there. You only need to know that it exists — and prefer to be there — to get there. Your healthy functioning allows you to live your life from moment to moment, always doing the best that you can. It allows you to remember that the most important aspect of life is enjoying it and feeling peaceful. When you feel this way, you are truly at your best, and everything tends to work itself out — and if it doesn't, you know that it also would have if you weren't engaged in healthy functioning.

Once you realize that healthy functioning is something that resides within you, and is every bit as real as any other part of your life, you can begin to call on it as a resource when you need it. You must, however, treat your healthy functioning as something that does exist; it must be more than an idea to you. It must be something you trust, like intuition.

Your Thought System versus Healthy Functioning

Your thought system is concerned only with the details of your life, how you compare with others, your worldly pursuits, your intellect, your ego gratification, and your endless supply of wants and needs. You can't satisfy your thought system. Its job is to think, compare, contrast and analyse. It is concerned with what happens in your life. The set of guidelines within which it operates is totally inconsistent with enjoyment. When you align yourself exclusively with your thought system, as so many people do, you are doomed to a life of frustration and unhappiness.

You can't think your way to happiness, nor can you do anything to make yourself happy. Happiness is a state of mind, not a set of circumstances. It's a peaceful feeling you can learn to live with, not something you have to search for. You can never find happiness by searching because the moment you try, you imply that it is found outside yourself. It isn't. Happiness is the feeling of your own healthy functioning. When you accept the idea that healthy functioning is a significant part of yourself, you can stop *trying* to be happy and simply *learn* to be happy.

If you don't learn to trust in and access your healthy functioning, it's impossible to learn to be happy, because rather than learning to look for a feeling within yourself, you will continue to pay attention to the negative thoughts that run through your mind.

Your healthy functioning is not concerned with what

happens in your life. It has a more expansive vision. It is concerned with *how you relate* to what happens in your life. Obviously there is a tremendous difference between these two modes. Your thought system comes up with what 'it thinks' would make it happy. Your healthy functioning, on the other hand, is what makes happiness possible. If all you had was your thought system, you would never be happy. You would be able to *think* of plenty of things that might make you happy, but you could never actually *feel* happy. Your thinking mind would keep coming up with conditions that would supposedly make you happy, but when the conditions were met, your thought system would begin to process all over again — coming up with new conditions that must be met. Your thought system will come up with ideas like, 'I'll be happy when my financial circumstances get better.' If you won the lottery, however, your thought system would start all over again: 'I wish the jackpot had been bigger,' or 'Oh no, what if I lose the money,' or 'What if they run out of money and can't pay me?' Such thoughts would again start to fill your head.

Your healthy functioning is that part of you that allows you to feel happy whether or not your financial circumstances are what you would like them to be. It's a place within you that always feels content. Your healthy functioning is not interested in what happens, it's only interested in how you feel and how you relate to what happens. All events, the good and bad, come and go. It is only your memory, your thinking, that keeps any event alive and relevant. The key to unlocking your inner happiness is to realize that *you* are the creator of those thoughts. Your healthy functioning is the part of you that knows that the true power in life is in the thinker — you — and not in the thoughts themselves.

Your healthy functioning is not just a theory or a

passive entity to be read about and then forgotten. It's a very real, positive and living force within you that you can learn to access. And as I have stated, you have already accessed it many times in the past, at those moments when everything felt just right. The key to eliminating unhappiness and replacing it with joyfulness is to learn to recognize healthy functioning when it *is* present in your life, and to help it grow and develop.

Your mental health can never be completely lost, it can only be covered up by negative, habitual and insecure thoughts that you have learned to take too seriously. The more seriously you take your own thoughts, the more distant your healthy functioning seems to be. Becoming aware that you have not just a personality and thoughts about your life, but also this other part of yourself, this 'healthy functioning', is a major weapon against unhappiness. When you know deep in your heart (even in the midst of a depressed state) that beneath your negativity lies a peaceful and light-hearted feeling that is ever present, you will regain the hope and confidence that a nicer, non-depressed, feeling is just around the corner — which it is. The only factor holding your unhappiness in place is your own thinking. All you need to do is relax and open your mind to the possibility that there is more to life than what you think about, and a new richness and sense of peace will begin to unfold for you. Begin by appreciating the simple, powerful feeling of your own healthy functioning.

If you are a parent, try to think back to the moment your first child was born. Remember the bliss, the joy in the way you felt. If you aren't a parent, remember an instance when you were completely 'present', a time when your mind was nowhere else but right where you were, a time when everything seemed 'just right'. It may have been a time in the beauty of nature, in a forest or by the sea. Perhaps it was a time when you fell in love. Everyone, no matter who they are, or how depressed they have been, has had at least some moments of healthy functioning in their life. No one had to teach you how to feel your own mental health. It just happens, all by itself, when you slow down your thinking and turn off your thinking mind. Your healthy functioning exists in the *now*. It occurs when you take your focus of attention off your concerns and problems, and instead allow your mind to feel at rest.

As you begin to realize that your healthy functioning comes from you and not from external sources, no matter how beautiful they may be, you can begin tapping into this beautiful place whenever you wish. Becoming conscious of your healthy functioning can be learned. You can learn to tap into it as easily while you are with your children or at work as you can while you are sitting in front of a fire or walking in a forest. All it takes is understanding, intention, patience, and practice.

Your healthy functioning is not only a place you can tap into on rare occasions or when you are sitting quietly by yourself, it's a place in which you can live. Ask yourself daily, even hourly, 'Where is that place in me? I know it's there because I've felt it before.' Your search for, and recognition of, your healthy functioning must be a significant and integral part of your life.

Your worldly pursuits, your dreams, and your aspirations are not jeopardized when you learn to tap into your healthy functioning. On the contrary, you will begin to see the bigger picture, you'll see what truly motivates you and what you really want in your life. You will also see what activities and pursuits would be better left alone. This ability to leave things alone will also be true with regard to your thinking. Once you see where a particular train of thought is leading you, and you don't like where you're headed, you'll be able to change course. You'll spend less time doing things mechanically, and more time doing things for the love of it. Instead of believing 'Anything worth doing is worth doing well,' you'll start to see that 'Anything worth doing is worth doing because you enjoy it.' You'll have authentic inner power, a greater ability to say 'no' when it's appropriate, and the wisdom to know what you *really* want. Accessing your healthy functioning allows you to see information in new and creative ways, and allows you to make rational, productive decisions in a timely manner. It allows you to enjoy, rather than struggle with, the ebbs and flows of life. It encourages your wisdom and common sense to surface.

Your healthy functioning can be pointed to and it can be felt. You can see the effects of its energy. You can see acts of loving kindness, compassion, and caring. You can see people who used to be angry and depressed who are now peaceful, loving, and happy. You can see people who have so much love and self-respect in their hearts that they rarely get defensive, upset, or critical of others.

Looking for the Clues

You can begin to look for clues to point you in the direction of your healthy functioning. To begin, you must first acknowledge that you have it in you — and then appreciate it when it is present. Don't just look for healthy functioning when you feel upset, but pay attention to it when you are feeling good. In this way, your healthy functioning can grow. As more and more of your energy and attention are directed towards this other part of yourself, you will find yourself experiencing it far more often. The better feeling you experience will feed on itself, giving you more confidence and more hope, setting forth a positive, life-enhancing cycle. Over time you will be able to see yourself moving in and out of your healthy functioning, and eventually you will be able to live in this state of mind most of the time. Even when you aren't able to tap into this happier state, you will at least know that it exists. This knowledge will protect and shield you against the grips of unhappiness and depression.

Your healthy functioning must become more important and more real to you than your unhappiness has been in the past. If it does, you will see new light and new hope emerging in your life. The moments of mental health you have experienced in the past will become minutes, then hours, and finally a way of life. If you can see the truth in what I am saying, that there is so much more to you than your unhappiness and your negative thoughts about yourself, you have reached the start of your road to freedom. You must begin to acknowledge that you do indeed have mental health, that you do have healthy functioning. You must realize that even if you don't feel it at the moment, it's still there, waiting for your attention.

Imagine that you have a special pair of orange socks that you have lost but would like to wear. If you are certain that you own them, and you know what they look like, and you really want to find them, then you are a thousand times more likely to find them than if you don't even know that you own them! How would you ever find something if you didn't even know what you were looking for — or for that matter that there was even anything to look for?

If you begin actively to search out, explore, and yearn for your own inner sanity, you *will* find what you are looking for. As your understanding and faith in the existence of your healthy functioning increases you will discover a better feeling surfacing. As this part of you that is *never depressed* is recognized and acknowledged, it will begin to conquer your unhappiness in the same way that sunlight will bring life to a plant that has been left in the dark. Light is more powerful than darkness. Healthy functioning is more powerful than unhappiness. Once your inherent mental health and happiness are acknowledged, they will be too powerful to remain an inactive force in your life. Once you recognize this feeling for what it is, it will become self-reinforcing until it overshadows any unhappiness that remains.

You don't find light by studying the dark. I know this sounds obvious, and to a certain degree, it is. But this common-sense way of approaching life is anything but common. More often than not, therapists and friends will get you to describe your pain and look at the implications of it and the 'reasons' behind it in an attempt to bring you to a state of peace. You will be asked to explore the parts of your past that were painful and to 'get in touch' with your negativity and your dark side. *If you are depressed, you are already in touch with your negativity.* To become happy, you need to travel in the other direction — towards your healthy functioning. Please don't misunderstand what I am saying: a good listener and a sympathetic ear can do wonders for the soul, and is a sign of a good friendship. I'm not attempting to place judgment or criticize typical therapeutic approaches and certainly not good friendships. Instead, I'm showing you how to decide for yourself what is going to bring you what you want in life. If you have a dark side, fine. Acknowledge it and move forward. Excessive thinking about your past and your problems will only convince you that you do, in fact, have good reasons to be upset and unhappy.

When a football player is taking a penalty kick and there are 15,000 fans in the crowd screaming for and against him, he must keep his eye on the goal and forget everything else. The very best football players do just that. The slightest wavering of attention usually results in a missed shot, and perhaps a lost game. A good athlete will practise and practise that which works. He will not dwell on past mistakes. He will not entertain self-doubting thoughts. He will acknowledge, then release the images of his past mistakes from his consciousness. Achieving mental health and happiness works in a similar fashion except that the stakes are much higher.

If you asked a hundred 'happy people' the secret of their success, *none* of them would say to you that they never feel negative emotions, or that they never have negative thoughts, or that their pasts were perfect. Virtually all of them, however, would tell you that even in the midst of their negativity they knew there was something better, something more important to them than the awful feeling they were experiencing at that moment. Their faith in this other part of themselves is the driving force behind their happiness. Happy people know there is something better, more powerful and more important than what they are thinking about! They know that studying their unhappiness won't bring them happiness.

In the chapters that follow I will be referring to your healthy functioning many times. You will be learning about tools that can enable you to tap into this nicer feeling more often in your life. As you read, keep in mind that your goal is to feel better. As you learn to dismiss the obstacles that interfere with your healthy functioning, you will be building a foundation of mental health that will last for a lifetime.

4

Dismissing Thoughts

The average person will have approximately 50,000 thoughts enter and leave her mind in any given day. Luckily, we have a very important ability — the ability to 'dismiss' thoughts as they enter our mind.

Dismissing thoughts is a natural, effortless process that keeps us from confusion, anxiety, overstimulation, and getting too caught up in our own thinking. Without this ability, we would undoubtedly all eventually suffer from nervous breakdowns and fall apart. There would simply be too much mental activity to handle.

Consider what you would do if you were enjoying a film on a Saturday evening when, during a slow moment, you began wondering whether you should paint your bedroom blue or white next summer. Chances are you would simply dismiss this thought from your mind, along with the other tens of thousands of thoughts that enter your mind during the course of a given day. There is little chance you would let this thought interfere with your enjoyment of the evening. You wouldn't evaluate, analyse, or dwell on the thought — there would be no effort involved — you would just let it drift away. And as the thought drifted away, you would bring your attention back to what you were doing — watching the film. It is helpful to see the ease with which you dismiss thoughts throughout the day.

And the important question to ask yourself is: If I can dismiss one thought why can't I dismiss another? The simple truth is that *you can dismiss any thoughts you believe you can dismiss.*

Think for a moment what would have happened if you hadn't dismissed the thought about which colour to paint the bedroom, and instead had focused your attention on it. Had this been the case, the thought would have taken on more significance in your mind, creating the potential to affect your well-being. As you thought about the issue of painting your room, you would have begun to feel the effects. The question of what colour would have led to a feeling of confusion, followed by any number of additional thoughts such as 'I can never make up my mind,' which would have brought on a feeling of frustration or anxiety. One thought would naturally lead to another and another unless and until you chose to drop the thoughts altogether.

It's surprising how little control you have over which thoughts enter your mind to begin with. It's as if thoughts just appear in your mind, almost randomly. Your power or control over your own thinking begins *after* the formation of a thought. It is *after* you have a thought that you have the choice of continuing to think about it — or let it drift away. Your ability to let your thoughts drift away will be tied to your understanding that thoughts, in and of themselves, have no power to hurt you. Thoughts are nothing more than images in your mind, and you can drop those images whenever you choose to do so.

We are constantly dismissing thoughts of all types whenever we deem them unnecessary or unimportant. It is our faulty judgment regarding what is unnecessary that gets us into trouble. For example, while we might dismiss the thought about painting the bedroom, we might *not* dismiss the thought about how bad life has become. We dismiss one thought as insignificant, yet we analyse another as if it had a life of its own. It doesn't. One thought can be just as easily dismissed as another. Ironically, it's far more important to dismiss the thought about how bad your life has become than an innocuous thought about the colour of your bedroom. Few of us realize, however, that we have this choice whenever we wish. As you practice the art of dismissing thoughts, you will see how easy it really is.

As we have seen, whenever we take a thought seriously, regardless of the content, we set ourselves up to experience the effects of that thought and to feel the emotions tied to it. Fortunately, the reverse is also true. As we learn to dismiss thoughts that are interfering with our emotional well-being, we begin to feel better. Feeling better, in turn, sets a new positive cycle in motion. The better we feel, the fewer negative thoughts enter our mind. As negative thoughts do happen to enter our mind, we casually dismiss them — and so on.

Imagine, for a moment, that you are sitting around feeling bad about your finances. You're thinking about how hard it is to make ends meet. Thoughts like 'I'll never get out of debt' are filling your mind. You're feeling sorry for yourself. Then, all of a sudden, you smell smoke coming from a downstairs flat. You know there are children living down there and you instantly jump out of your chair and run downstairs to see if you can help. The questions to ask yourself are: What happened to your thoughts during the fire? Where did they go? Very simply, you dismissed them. You decided that dealing with the potential fire was more important than continuing to think about your debts. It's really that simple. Note that as soon as you dismissed the thoughts and went on to something else, you were free of the negative effects of those thoughts. You were no longer feeling sorry for yourself. You were re-energized, you even had the wherewithal to help in a crisis. Any negative feelings you had drifted away and were replaced by the feelings associated with your new thoughts.

The only way to bring back those same negative feelings you were experiencing regarding your personal finances is to begin thinking about the same things again. This might seem crazy but, interestingly enough, there are people who will do just that. In this case, they would deal with the fire, and then quickly return to their previous preoccupation. It's as though they would say to themselves, 'Now, where was I before I was interrupted? Oh, that's right, I was thinking about how bad my life has become. Yes, my life is really bad. And I feel really bad.' It might seem like I'm exaggerating, but truthfully, many of us will emotionally torture ourselves with our own thinking — without ever realizing that *we are doing it to ourselves.* This self-torture is totally absurd, yet so many people do it.

The moment you realize what you are doing to yourself is the moment you begin to set yourself free. *You are the thinker who is thinking about how bad your life is.* The power to stop doing this is in your hands. All you have to do is realize that you are the producer of your own thoughts. The thoughts themselves have no life of their own and can't harm you. Once forgotten, they are gone until you think of them again.

Human beings have a natural ability to disengage themselves from pointless and destructive thinking. For example, what happens to the office bickering when the boss suddenly comes through the door? Everyone instantly puts on their best behaviour. To do this, they *must* forget the arguing. The individuals involved are motivated to drop the thinking that was keeping the fight alive. However, it is often the case that if someone were to suggest to these same people that if they drop the thoughts the friction will be gone, the response will be something like, 'Easier said than done. We can't stop thinking about it.' While it sometimes seems as though this is the case, in reality it is not. The truth is that we are constantly dismissing thoughts but are usually unaware that we are doing it. It's important to know that you, like the office workers in the example, have a great deal of motivation to start dismissing thoughts that are making you unhappy. If you do, you will be happy and your problems will resolve themselves.

The Time Factor

If we consider the way most people get over problems and painful events, by far the most popular is the 'passage of time'. We have been taught to believe that 'time heals all wounds'. People rarely realize, however, that *they themselves* stopped perpetuating their problem by dropping it from thought. This 'dismissal' *is* the factor that brought their mental health back to them. Had they recognized this fact, it would be possible to maintain a high degree of mental health on an ongoing basis. But because this fact is overlooked, even when people do manage to regain some degree of mental health by dropping their thoughts, their lack of understanding of how they *actually* obtained their relief, makes it nearly impossible to hold on to their more positive feeling. Very simply, the next time negative thoughts (the same thoughts or new ones) enter their minds, they will be just as likely to fall victim to the same pattern. Rather than dismissing the thoughts as they come up, thereby regaining a more peaceful outlook, they will continue to engage the thoughts. Once a person learns that the secret of mental health is the dismissal of negative thoughts, he is free to experience mental health regularly.

The passage of time has no real relevance in helping us to get over something other than encouraging us to think about other things besides whatever is bothering us. As we have seen, we have the capacity to drop thoughts instantly when we are motivated and choose to do so. An understanding of thought allows us to see that all thoughts are just thoughts and all memory is just memory — whether something happened ten years ago or ten minutes ago. And as we begin to feel better by dismissing thoughts at will, the process gets easier. If the passage of time were really the determining factor that enabled a person to get over something, then all of us would get over things in an identical period of time. But we know this isn't the case.

This understanding has significant practical implications. Whereas we might have set up artificial cultural or social time frames to get over or recover from a situation, we can now see that it's entirely up to us. For example, if we tried something and failed, there is no preset period of time in which we can expect to get over it and move on. If it usually takes us a week to get over some sort of failure, it only means that seven days after an event we stop thinking about it and move on. Since the incident is now over and continues to exist only in our mind, if we want to we can stop paying attention to the thoughts we have about the incident, and instead dismiss the thoughts as they enter our mind. Once we discover how nice it is to feel better as a result of dismissing negative and painful thoughts, holding on to these thoughts becomes less and less appealing. Dismissing thoughts isn't something you have to learn, it's something you already do.

5

Wisdom

Certainly one of the questions I am most frequently asked is: If my thoughts are just thoughts, and they aren't something I have to be overly concerned with, then how do I know which thoughts to pay attention to and which thoughts to dismiss?

We are fortunate to have within us an inner intelligence that is deeper and more profound than any test could measure — wisdom. Your wisdom will tell you when to listen to and trust your thoughts and when to ignore them. It will tell you when you are thinking in a habitual, business-as-usual way and when you are thinking from a wise state of common sense.

Wisdom exists *outside* the confines of our individual thought system. In other words, when we tap into wisdom, we aren't thinking in a business-as-usual sense, but from an entirely different standpoint, which probably explains why so few people acknowledge their own wisdom. While as a society we have traditionally revered intelligence, it's important to know that wisdom does not come from thought alone; it isn't linked to your ability to use your intelligence or your memory. You can't 'figure out' what your wisdom is trying to tell you. Instead you learn to trust a quiet inner voice that knows what you need to know. And what's more, when it doesn't know an answer, it knows that it doesn't know.

Wisdom is your sense of knowing, an intuitive feeling that you have experienced many times. For instance, when you learn to drive a car, you never forget how to do so. You can stop driving for a number of months, or even years, then get in the driver's seat and drive perfectly. Wisdom is the internal knowing that allowed you to drive without having to relearn.

Wisdom exists in every aspect of your life. There are times when you simply know what is right for you, or when you know you can do something. This is quite different from having to think in search of an answer. To demonstrate the difference, think of an old friend. Do you have to come up with reasons why you love this person? Of course not. Your sense of knowing tells you who to love and who to avoid. Now think of someone you don't care for. If you're honest, you'd probably be able to list ten positive characteristics about this person. If you can't, I'll bet someone else can. The point is this: if you can list positive traits about a person, then why don't you like that person? Simply because your intuitive sense knows what is best for you. Your wisdom is far more powerful and all-knowing than your thinking mind.

I've already said that your thoughts aren't real. But if this is so, which thoughts should you pay attention to and which should you avoid? Very simply, your wisdom, your sense of knowing will tell you. Here is an example. You are in a bad mood and you have the following thought about your spouse: 'He's completely useless!' Do you dismiss this thought or not? The answer is yes. By dismissing this negative thought you avoid having a hundred additional thoughts about your husband that are going to lower your spirits — and get in the way of your wisdom! By dismissing the thought, you avoid having to feel bad, which is exactly what would happen if you continued to think negatively about your husband. How you feel is a function of your own thoughts. If you think negatively about your husband, you suffer — not your husband. By maintaining a positive feeling in your life and not being seduced by your negative thoughts, you keep the door open for your sense of knowing. Whenever you are in a positive feeling state, your healthy functioning — your wisdom — is at work.

What if your husband really is useless? What if, in a happier state of mind, something within you is telling you that some changes need to be made? Terrific! That's your inner wisdom at work. By all means listen to this voice and act upon it. *Wisdom is the quiet voice that speaks to you when you are feeling good, when you are happy, when you have your bearings.* In this case, it would be the sense of *knowing* that something needs to change in your marriage. This sense of knowing didn't come from thinking poorly about your husband and it certainly didn't come from feeling bad. *Wisdom never comes from negativity nor can it exist when your mind is filled with negative thoughts.* Your wisdom comes from quietening down, from dismissing your negative thoughts — even though those thoughts pertained to your husband — and listening to your inner knowing. This identical process is always available to you when you quieten down and open up to it. Your wisdom will always speak to you if one simple condition is met: dismiss all negative thoughts surrounding the issue and quieten down. The answer will be there.

William James, the father of modern psychology, said, 'Wisdom is seeing something in a non-habitual manner.' Wisdom is seeing an old problem in a new, fresh way. When you discover your wisdom you will free yourself from your fixed and habitual patterns of thinking and be able to navigate yourself towards a life of happiness and inner peace. Your wisdom is all you need. It will become the steering wheel that tells you when to move forward and when to take a step back, listen, and wait for an answer.

Wise people throughout history have been those who saw that while life is real, life's problems are an illusion, they are thought-created. These people know that we manufacture and blow problems way out of proportion through our own ability to think. They also know that if we can step outside the boundaries of our own thinking, we can find the answer we are looking for. This, in a nutshell, is wisdom: the ability to see an answer without having to think of an answer. Wisdom is the 'ah ha, that's so obvious' experience most of us have had many times. Few people seem to understand that this voice is always available to us.

Wisdom is indeed your inner sense of knowing. It is true mental health, a peaceful state of mind where answers to questions are as plentiful as the problems you see when you aren't experiencing wisdom. It's as if wisdom lies in the space between your thoughts, in those quiet moments when your 'biological computer' is turned off. Here is an example.

Mark was (and is) a very intelligent person. His usual pattern was to think and talk about his problems in an attempt to overcome them. He felt that because his problems were 'real', he was justified in trying to solve them. On the surface this seems rational, that is, until you realize that problems are thought-related. In other words, the act of thinking about your problems is the mechanism that keeps them alive and makes them seem real. To see this another way, try this experience. Stop reading for a moment and think of a problem in your life. There it is, right in front of you. An interesting question to ask yourself is: where was the problem a moment ago, before you thought about it? It wasn't with you because you weren't thinking about it. This doesn't mean there aren't issues in your life that need addressing, but it does suggest that those issues aren't 'problems' unless they are present in your mind.

Mark felt he needed a career change. He was bored, frustrated, disappointed with the politics of his company, disappointed with his co-workers, disappointed with his pay, and so forth. He spent an enormous amount of time by himself, with friends, his wife, even a career counsellor, discussing and thinking about in great detail what he didn't like about his job.

Mark desperately wanted an answer. He wanted to know what he should do instead, where he should turn, who he should talk to, what he would rather be doing. Each day he would review what he didn't like about his job. Then, upon returning home, he would go over it again with his wife. He was racking his brain for a solution.

Mark felt, as do most people, that if thoughts came to his mind, he should study and analyse them to see what he could find. He experienced his ability to think as something that was happening *to* him rather than as something that *he was doing*. There is, of course, a major difference between these two perceptions. If you perceive your thinking as something that is happening *to* you, you are a victim of it; thinking seems to be something that is imposed upon you that requires you to think about it some more. You become so caught up in your own thinking that you lose the ability to access your wisdom. This process becomes an endless loop whereby you never realize that you are looking for an answer in the very place where the problem lies. If, however, you perceive correctly that thinking is something that originates *within* you, that thinking is something that you are doing, moment to moment, then life looks quite different. In this case, you can see yourself as the one doing the thinking; you can remain completely detached from the content of your thinking, which enables you to gain some perspective. You find that instead of being lost in your own thoughts, you feel a sense of spaciousness, balance, and perspective. You see beyond the confines of your thought-created world to what is really true in the moment.

Mark needed to know that as thoughts came to his mind he had the option of whether or not to follow those thoughts. It took some time to convince him that it was in his best interest to stop thinking about the issue of his career altogether. He needed to rediscover the positive feelings that had brought him into his chosen field to begin with. As he did so, he regained his perspective and realized that, although there were aspects of his job that were less than perfect, it was in his best interest to postpone his new job search until he had completed a long-term project to which he had committed himself.

A year later Mark realized that the best decision he had ever made was not leaving the firm at the time he most wanted to. Eventually he did leave it, moving on to a related but better job with almost twice the pay. He said he never would have been able to get his new job if he hadn't proved himself by completing the project he was working on at his original firm. Mark's thinking had earned him only a great deal of frustration; his wisdom earned him a new job.

Wisdom is your healthy functioning in action. It's a tool that you can use to guide you through life. Wisdom is more useful and powerful than your 'normal' thinking. It can answer any question you may have. Whenever you are confronted with a question or problem, clear your mind, quieten down, and ask your wisdom for an answer. You may be surprised at what you receive.

6

Thoughts Grow with Attention

Your past is now only a figment of your imagination, and so is your future. The only moment that is real is right now. As you recognize the powerful part that your thinking plays in creating your experience you begin to realize that life is not responsible for your happiness or unhappiness, your thoughts are. This is a powerful insight because it suggests that you alone are capable of changing your own life. American philosopher Ralph Waldo Emerson once said, 'The ancestor to every action is a thought.' You must realize that to become a happier person, you must first imagine that it's possible.

The way you feel is determined by your thoughts. The more attention you put on anything that is negative, the worse you will feel. Again, I ask that you use your own wisdom and common sense to decide whether or not to believe me. Despite the popular idea that talking about and working through negative emotions is a good idea, I'm suggesting that common sense dictates otherwise. People have been 'working through' endless negative emotions for years now, and very few are much better off than when they started. The questions to ask yourself (and your therapist) are: when does the analysis stop? When have I had enough? When do I get to feel better?

If you believe that your thoughts are real — and you

are encouraged to work through the worst of them — you will end up with even more to contend with, because the more you think, the bigger and more important the thoughts will seem, and the more of them there will be to deal with. Because your feelings are determined by what you think about, you will, by necessity, sink even lower. And unfortunately, because you are feeling lower, you will now think even more negative thoughts, new ones that you now have to 'work through'. It's an endless negative spiral that never takes you upward towards where you want to be — happy. The spiral will end when you decide that enough is enough. It will end when you start with a clean slate, with a clear mind, and when you realize that the only thing holding your unhappiness in place is your own thinking. If you really want to be happy, you must stop focusing on your negative feelings, and start looking for the magical feeling of healthy functioning that resides inside you.

Troubleshooting

Troubleshooting is a way of life for many people. It means being on the look out for what's wrong, finding flaws, seeking out imperfections, pointing out potential pitfalls, finding fault, generating concerns, being a sceptic, and remembering mistakes. For a computer product this can be crucial; for a human being it can be devastating.

Troubleshooting is a socially acceptable form of mental illness. Many people are proud of their ability to predict potential problems, see fault in others, and remember past mistakes. They call themselves 'realists'. They consider their fault-finding skills necessary and important. They rationalize their behaviour and way of thinking by saying such things as, 'You must learn from history,' and 'Someone has to look out for the problems.'

Troubleshooters often raise children with low self-esteem. They are so busy pointing out the ways that their children could improve that they totally forget to enjoy their presence. The children often interpret their parents' attitude to mean that they are not good enough. Troubleshooters have low self-esteem themselves. Rather than experiencing what is happening in their lives, they are constantly thinking of ways to improve their experience. Regardless of how good things get, they constantly want more.

A troubleshooter can *never* be satisfied because she is using her thinking against herself. She is too busy evaluating her life to enjoy it. She picks up the slightest imperfections and turns them into a big deal. Even when she likes something, she compares it to something else.

There is certainly nothing wrong with wanting to improve, excel, achieve, or compare. But there *is* something harmful to the human psyche when, instead of being open and receptive to the beauty of life, it is overflowing with comparisons, criticisms, suggestions, and thoughts of imperfections. Life doesn't have to be a contest to see how many flaws you can find. Life can be beautiful, and it will be, when you start dismissing the thoughts you have that take you away from a good feeling about life, a feeling of love and appreciation, your healthy psychological functioning. Instead of following the troubleshooting thoughts you have, practise ignoring them. Rather than following through with an unnecessary suggestion to someone, practise holding your tongue. Instead, offer your support for doing it their own way. Instead of anticipating potential problems and reviewing past mistakes, keep yourself here, in this moment. See for yourself how living moment to moment tends to take care of most problems. Remind yourself that your inner wisdom and healthy functioning will learn from history — all by itself — even if you don't review your mistakes in your head. Watch what happens when you dismiss a concern in your mind as 'just a thought'. Notice how very few of your concerns actually manifest into significant real-life problems. For those concerns that really do become problems, watch how gracefully you solve them when you remain present and focused, when your head isn't muddled with a lot of other thoughts, related or not, that only add to the problem.

The process of a troubleshooter's thinking is very easy to explain. She looks at something or someone and thoughts begin to bubble. The specific content of her thoughts aren't important. What ends up hurting her is the nature of her thinking, the fact that her thoughts are seeking to improve the person, place, or thing. Rather than dismissing those thoughts, as a happier person would tend to do, the troubleshooter pays attention to her thoughts, believing them to be real. Because she thinks her thoughts are so important, she either points them out to someone or keeps thinking them to herself. The thoughts feed on one another and begin to take on a life of their own. She feels that she wouldn't have thought them up if they weren't worthy of concern.

A happy person might have the very same thoughts enter his mind, but the way he would respond to those thoughts would be quite different. The thoughts would bubble to the surface. He would then acknowledge that he was thinking them, dismiss them, and go on with his day. Obviously, if his wisdom told him that any particular thoughts did have merit, and the issue was important, he would choose to do something about the situation. He wouldn't however, allow his mind to blow the situation out of proportion. He would tap into his healthy functioning as best he could, knowing that his wisdom would provide him with the answers he needs.

He would remember a golden rule of happiness: *it's impossible to feel gratitude for something when you are too busy trying to improve it.*

The Past

To break free from unhappiness you have to bring yourself back to the present. You must realize that your past is no longer here — it's over. It exists only within your own thinking. It was real then, but now, it's only a part of your imagination.

From generation to generation, each of us has been taught that the past represents what is, and that is predicts the future. A person who is psychologically sound and of good judgment is seen to look carefully to the past when thinking of future plans. Therefore, it makes sense to most people to recall the past when dealing with something in the present. This tendency, however, while useful at times, can wreak havoc on our rapport with others. It also takes us away from our healthy functioning.

The truth is that many arguments, painful confrontations, or difficult situations are only difficult because the people involved are busy thinking about the past without realizing they are doing so! In other words they are filtering their present moments through thoughts of the past.

On the surface, almost everyone realizes the past is over. Very few, however, internalize this understanding deeply enough to prevent the past from haunting them. Instead, they allow thoughts of the past to contaminate the present, interfering with the present experience of healthy functioning. If you can remember that the past is only a memory, you will be able to ignore, to a very large degree, the thoughts of the past that get in the way of enjoying life. You can learn a great deal from your past, but you need not suffer because of it. Your

understanding of thought will allow you to remain
right here, in the present moment, where happiness can
exist.

7

Thought Systems

Once you have a clear understanding of the dynamics of thought — what it is, who's doing it, and what happens as a result — you are ready to learn exactly what it is that holds your negative thinking in place, what keeps it hanging around in your mind.

All of us, from the time we are infants, have a natural desire to make sense of life. We relate facts, compare events, and form conclusions out of what we see. This is a very natural process; we need to create at least some order in our lives and to learn from our mistakes and circumstances.

The way we go about making sense of our lives is to organize our thoughts into what is called a 'thought system'. A thought system is a self-contained thinking unit through which we interpret the world. It is almost like a pair of sunglasses that we never take off, and it is through these glasses that we see the relative significance or lack of it in everything we are exposed to. For example, if you grew up in a family where there was a huge emphasis on money, where virtually every dinner conversation centred around the subject, you will have that information stored in your thought system. You will therefore be predisposed to placing an enormous emphasis on money yourself. When a friend asks you to go shopping with her, you might find

yourself wondering 'How much money will I spend?'
or 'How much money will I need to bring?' It becomes
'normal' for you to look at life in that particular way.
Because your thought system is filled up with certain
types of information, you simply never question your
own way of looking at life — it just seems right to you.

Let me make one thing perfectly clear: there's nothing
wrong with your thought system. The way it developed
was innocent. You were simply given a set of facts that
were represented as 'truth', and unless you are a very rare
exception to the human species, you bought the
information, hook, line, and sinker. What else could you
do? You were a child eager to learn about life. When
your parents and other important role models gave you
information you accepted it as truthful. Over time, you
stored this so-called truth in your memory until you
could see life in no other way, all the while developing
conditioned responses to certain information that seem
appropriate to you. An example could be your tendency
to feel threatened or defensive when someone makes a
suggestion about something you're doing. There is
nothing inherent in the words people use when they
speak to you that makes you feel this way; it's your
thought system that interprets the words and gives
them meaning to you. Over time you (and everyone
else) make 'cause and effect' relationships between
events and reactions that you consider natural. So
instead of saying to yourself, 'I get really defensive over
nothing,' you will react in a defensive way and think
nothing of it. Every human being, no matter how wise
or happy she is, has at least some made-up cause-and-
effect relationships that she will call normal. When
something upsets *us*, it seems likely to us that it would
upset others too. It takes a great deal of understanding
and humility to realize that an upset comes from your
own thinking and not from the things you are thinking

about. It takes a great deal of wisdom to realize that your conditioned responses are just that — they are conditioned, they are learned, they are made up from your own thinking.

To compound the problem, thought systems have a very strong, almost insidious tendency to validate themselves. Because your thought system is filled with information from your own past, it looks for examples to prove to itself that it is 'right'. Let's suppose that you grew up in a family where it was readily accepted that people were generally selfish. Your parents were always pointing out people's faults, bad habits, self-centred tendencies, and so on. If this belief was in your thought system, you would tend to notice people pushing and shoving in queues, stealing from one another, and being less than giving. If, on the other hand, you grew up in a family where it was taught that people are generally kind to one another, and this belief was ingrained in your thought system, you would have an entirely different outlook on life. You would tend to notice the good in people, the kind things that people do for one another, the way that people band together after traumatic events, and so forth.

Notice that I use the word *tend* in describing what you see as a result of your thought system. It's not that you would never see the good in people if you were taught to see the bad, or that you would never see the bad if you were taught the opposite, it's just that you would be predisposed to notice that which you were taught.

When you look at it objectively, you can see the innocence in the development of a thought system. You can trace your own thought system back many generations to your great great grandparents, and well before them. In a real sense, you see that which you were taught to see. Over time, and through many years of validation and selective perception based on what you were taught, you made a series of conclusions about life. The sum total of all of your conclusions can be called your attitude.

Your attitude about life can be summarized as a series of thoughts that you have come to believe as truth. There is nothing holding your attitude in place other than your own thinking. Your attitude is not in your genes. If it were, your attitude would be similar to other members of your family in the same way that hair or eye colour usually is. Attitude is not due to your circumstances. If it were, positive attitudes would be tied to positive circumstances and negative attitudes would be tied to difficult circumstances. We all know this isn't the case. There are many examples of people who live in what seem to be easy circumstances who act as though they are victims, and there are equal numbers of people who appear to have nothing at all, yet seem to be delighted by nothing more than the gift of life.

Because of the self-validating nature of your thought system, you will always be tempted to continue thinking in the way that you are accustomed. After all, you are predisposed to a certain way of thinking. But being predisposed doesn't have to mean you fall into the trap. There are many people who are predisposed to being overweight who are thin; many who are predisposed to certain illnesses who never get sick; and thousands who are predisposed to unhappiness who are happy, productive people. Once you see how little there is holding your thinking in place, you can begin to distrust your own thoughts. Your thoughts are not based on absolute truth; they are contaminated by your thought system — your individual version of life — in the same way that my thoughts are contaminated by my individual version of life.

The difference between a happy person and an

unhappy person lies, to a very large degree, in their humility. A happy person is able to admit to himself that the way he sees life isn't set in stone. It's not that the way he sees life has no merit, but a happy person understands that his attitude is self-made. In other words, it is based solely on selective perception and learned experience. An unhappy person, on the other hand, is far more stubborn. He is certain that his thinking really means something and he is determined to prove it. He will show you (at the expense of his own well-being) that life really is as bad as he says it is. He will point to endless examples to prove his position and, of course, he will be right.

Because your thought system is so familiar to you, it will always seem to be giving you accurate information about the way life really is. When your thought system tells you, 'Life isn't very good' or any other self-defeating message, it will seem to be telling you the truth. It takes a very strong and wise person to distrust his own thinking. The good news is that when you stop paying attention to your thought system, and when you aren't using your ability to think against yourself, you are left with your healthy psychological functioning. Because healthy functioning is your most natural state of mind, all you have to do is avoid the mental processes that interfere with healthy functioning.

Imagine that you had a huge cork at the bottom of the sea and you let go of it. What would happen? The cork would shoot straight up, naturally rising to the surface unless something got in its way. In the case of a cork, it might be seaweed, coral, or rocks that prohibited it from reaching its final destination.

Your healthy functioning is just like that cork except that it resides at the centre of your being. Your healthy functioning wants nothing more than to spring to the surface in the form of high self-esteem and a happy life.

Your healthy functioning will do just that unless something gets in its way — and the only potential source of interference is your negative thinking. Disregard the negative thoughts you have about yourself and your healthy functioning will begin to fulfill its mission.

Ego

The concept of ego is very closely related to that of a thought system. Both are thought-created. The truth is that human beings don't even have egos — there is no such thing. People only have egos because they think they do. Your ego is your idea or thoughts about who you are. The popular notion that people need an ego to live and succeed in life is untrue. We can only begin to appreciate who we truly are when we lessen our need to prove ourselves. As we let go of our thoughts of who we are, our insecurity begins to lift. It is then that we can begin to live *outside* our thought system or ego. It is then that we connect with our healthy functioning.

As a person drops insecure thinking patterns, he begins to experience his natural feeling of self-esteem, the feeling of gratitude for what we are rather than what we are doing. Without the pressure of having to maintain our ego (who we think we are), we are more able to relax and enjoy whatever we happen to be doing at the moment. We find that we are able to be touched by the little things in life that we used to overlook. We also begin to notice that we feel the happiest when we think about ourselves the least often.

Don't be concerned that as you drop your ego from your life you will become passive or apathetic, because you won't. In fact, just the opposite will happen. As you free yourself from the bondage of your limiting belief structure, you become far more interested in life and all it has to offer. Dropping your ego allows you to see new options and alternatives that were previously invisible. For example, if you drop the idea about yourself that you are a shy person, you might find that you really do like to communicate with other people. A client of mine recently decided to do just this, and she has just planned the first party she has ever hosted. If you begin to ignore, even a little, the thoughts you have about what you like and don't like, you might be willing to try new things, go to an evening class, start an exercise programme, eat at a new restaurant. It all starts from the willingness to see yourself as more than what you have defined yourself to be.

Fred is a 45-year-old man whose wife died of cancer. He entered therapy because he felt that he had mourned deeply and for a long time the loss of his wife, and now he wanted to feel happy again. He found his therapist through the phone book. He was quickly diagnosed by his therapist as 'chronically depressed'. Unfortunately, Fred deeply respected doctors and he accepted this diagnosis in the absolute sense of the word. To him, 'chronic' meant 'forever'. He began thinking of himself as depressed and entered a support group for depressed people who wished to share their experiences. Fred's next year was very painful. His self-image was built on a foundation of thoughts about himself as depressed. He looked for and found evidence to support this diagnosis. He remembered incidents from his past when he had been depressed. He became isolated from society and hid himself in his home for fear that his depression might get worse.

Then Fred came to see me. Fred had never been told that his own thoughts were shaping his view of himself and his attitude toward life. His earlier therapy had convinced him that he was a victim of depression, which he would have to fight for the rest of his life. His own interpretation of his diagnosis left him in little doubt that his doctor was right. The more he thought about depression the worse he felt, which only convinced him and his therapist that the original diagnosis was correct.

In our sessions together, Fred learned how his thoughts shaped his perceptions and led to his feelings. He quickly came to the correct conclusion that he had been fighting an impossible battle. 'How could I ever feel better,' he asked, 'by believing my thoughts about myself as a chronically depressed person?' He realized that he had been trapped within the confines of his own thinking, yet he was attempting to use that same thinking to get away from his depression. This would be like using matches to put out a fire.

This simple realization led Fred to a series of insights into his own thought system. He realized that he had been using his own thinking against himself his entire lifetime and had rarely questioned his beliefs. He realized that he had unknowingly lived his life completely absorbed in the content of his own thoughts. Today, Fred lives an ordinary life as a happy, productive person.

8

Choice Points

Life can be seen as a continuing series of 'choice points'. The sum of our decisions regarding the direction we take with our choice points will determine, to a very large extent, the way we feel.

A choice point is an isolated moment in time when you have an opportunity to choose between your healthy functioning (the path of love and contentment) and the path of 'thinking it through'. The following chart describes the two paths:

Path of Love (Healthy Functioning)	Path of Thinking It Through
Seeing the truth and moving on	Trying to 'get to the bottom'
Choosing love and forgiveness	Choosing anger
Not dwelling on the issue	Dwelling on the issue
Happiness rather than being right	Being right is important
Letting go	Hanging on
Thinking is light and diffuse	Thinking is complicated
Little or no analysis	Thorough analysis
It's OK	It's not OK
I don't need to get into it	I need to get into it

It's OK that we disagree	I need to prove myself
No need to have a firm opinion	I must express my opinion

Every time a thought enters your mind, or something happens in your life, it's a new opportunity for you. Do you take the path of healthy functioning, or do you take the road of pain? How are you going to respond? Is it worth giving up your mental health and happiness to follow a path of pain, of thinking it through, simply because you are familiar with it? These are the important questions that must be addressed if you want to stop following the path that ultimately leads to unhappiness and depression.

Let's suppose your father says something that you wish he hadn't — this is a choice point. Your sink starts leaking for the third time this month — another choice point. Your spouse criticizes the way you handle the family budget — another one. In each of these examples, and tens of thousands of others like them, you have a moment in which a decision must be made.

If your father says something you wish he hadn't, you can take the path of thinking it through. You can think to yourself, 'Why did he say that to me?' (getting to the bottom of it) and 'It makes me furious when he does that' (choosing anger). You can then dwell on what he said, think of all the reasons he said it, and all the things you would like to say to him if you 'had the guts'. You can get really into it. You can talk about it, think about it some more, express your anger, figure it out, and even talk to a therapist about how it makes you feel. Is this road justified? It is if you want it to be. You must, however, become conscious of exactly where this road is going to take you. The extent to which you follow this path will determine just how bad you will feel. The reason so many people stick to this path is because they know of no other. When they are on this path, they feel bad, and because they feel bad, it seems as though the world is causing their misery, so they think about it some more. The tendency here is to imagine that if you think it through thoroughly enough, you will somehow feel better, and a vicious cycle continues. But feeling better is *not* a part of this path. On this path you are putting your attention and energy on the problem or on what you don't like about your life. This is not a source of satisfaction in your life.

I don't mean to suggest, however, that this path is never appropriate. Sometimes you really *do* need to think things through, analyse, compare, and even 'get to the bottom of it'. Sometimes it is appropriate to get angry and express your feelings. But this is not often the way to go if what you are looking for is happiness.

The path of healthy functioning is nothing more than *not taking* the path of thought. When you're on the path of healthy functioning you have a built-in protection against depression — while knowing exactly what will happen if you go the other way. Choosing the path of mental health is a decision to respond to life in a way that allows a feeling of happiness to permeate your life, instead of reacting to every negative thought that enters your mind.

Let's return for a moment to our example of your father saying something to you that you wish he hadn't. If you were to choose the path of healthy functioning, this is what you would do: as soon as your head began to fill up with negative thoughts and questions about your father and his motives, you would *immediately recognize that you were thinking!* That recognition alone would alert you to the fact that you were now at risk of using your own thinking against yourself. You would begin monitoring your own thinking, not allowing your head to fill up with negative thoughts. As negative thoughts entered your mind, you would dismiss them. You would know that allowing yourself to focus on the negative thoughts would only hurt you — it would take you *away from* your healthy functioning. Here's the benefit to you: with each negative thought that you dismissed from your mind, a nicer feeling within you would take its place. As you felt better, you would regain your perspective and you would know exactly what to do next. You would either take some action such as discussing the issue with your father with a calm and loving attitude, or you would simply dismiss his comments and decide that it's really not that important. This entire process only takes a second and it all stems from knowing that you have a choice. Each time you practise this conscious choice-making you will get better at choosing your healthy functioning — and you will decide that feeling good is worth the choice.

Your Feelings

Your feelings are with you, not to be studied and dealt with, but to let you know that you are at another choice point. You can use this choice point as an opportunity to become more conscious, more loving, and happier. You can use it to solidify your faith in your healthy functioning, or you can ignore the fact that you are at a choice point and react to your feelings as if they were your enemy, something to fear.

Your feelings are your tip off, your internal warning signal that you are on the wrong path. If your feeling is negative, it tells you that it's time to redirect your energy and attention towards your healthy functioning. This is where an understanding that you have healthy functioning becomes critical. If you know that there is a part of yourself that is never depressed, never unhappy, ever-understanding, and filled with compassion towards yourself, it puts you in a position to direct your energy and attention towards that part. Without this knowledge, finding your happiness is a lot like washing your clothes in dirty water. You can't find happiness within your unhappiness — you must look for it in a place beyond your thinking mind.

When you understand that you have choice points, you can feel a negative emotion such as anger, but at the same moment you can be fully aware that another part of yourself would prefer to respond with love and peace instead of anger. When you become grounded in this truth, you will begin to look for this better feeling even in midst of your negativity. The more certain you are that your healthy functioning does exist, independent of your depression, the more patient and persistent you will be in your search. Like a tree in a forest reaching for sunshine, you will seek out a part of you that is peaceful. And when you find that part of yourself, no matter how small it may be, you will put all of your attention on that feeling, thus giving it what it needs to grow and develop.

Choice point after choice point you will become stronger and more committed to your own healthy functioning. Each time you choose happiness over negativity you will be a little bit closer to conquering your depression. This is not an easy path to take because habits are hard to break. But look at your options — they are not easy either. If instead of becoming aware of your choice points and choosing love over negativity you continue using your thinking against yourself, you will continue to live a life of pain.

Every moment of your life is another choice point, another fork in the road. Even when you are feeling good, you are at a choice point. You could, after all, make a different choice and focus your attention on negativity. You probably wouldn't do this intentionally, but you might do it precisely because your life is an ongoing series of choice points.

An Example of Choice Points in the Work Place
An excellent example of how you can use choice points in your life comes from a client of mine who came to me for stress management that related to her job. She managed a division of a large company and was responsible for overseeing the activities of a few dozen employees. The problem was this: every single day she would become overwhelmed by the stress. She would react to her angry and frustrated thoughts and ended up alienating her employees. This happened so often that her employees actually became frightened by the sight of her. They felt distant and resentful. Production was falling and everyone in the office was frustrated.

When my client learned that her own thinking was the source of her frustration, she began to see her choice points. She learned that she could choose to follow her angry trains of thought, or she could recognize what was happening and wait for it to pass. In her own words, 'I began to see how often angry thoughts would fill my head. I learned that instead of reacting to those thoughts, I could simply take a deep breath and do the best I could to clear my mind. I knew that if I didn't engage myself in the thoughts I was having they would begin to dissipate. As my negative thoughts disappeared I would regain my perspective and sense of well-being and everything would be OK again. To be honest with you, to this day some of the same thoughts I always had still enter my mind — the difference now is that I know they are only thoughts. I have a different kind of relationship to them. I don't have to react to them any more simply because they are in my head.'

My client learned how to feel when her self-destructive thoughts were entering and filling her head. She learned to detect this feeling earlier and earlier so that the accumulation wouldn't get very far. She knew that her choice point was that moment when she first felt the negativity arising. She could, of course, choose to engage her thoughts, which so many people do, and become more frustrated and further lose her perspective, or she could take a breath, dismiss her thoughts and wait for a more peaceful feeling to return. Needless to say, her employees noticed a significant change. They were no longer frightened. Production went up, in fact, higher than it had ever been before. As important, my client began to enjoy her job and the people she worked with again. She also learned that the same practice applies to every part of her life, not just her career. She learned to use her choice points in her relationships with her husband, her children, and her friends.

It's important to know that my client was not sweeping problems under the carpet. On the contrary, she was learning to deal with problems in a more productive way. Everyone makes better decisions and solves problems more efficiently when they are not immobilized by their own thinking. Try it for yourself. The next time you feel yourself reacting to your own thoughts, dismiss them. Clear your mind and search for your healthy functioning. Don't worry, the problem will still be there, but you will notice how much easier it is to deal with any problem when you have your bearings and keep your perspective. Many problems that once felt like emergencies will now seem like minor irritations.

◈9◈

The Thinking Habit

Whether you're trying to stop drinking alcohol or smoking cigarettes, cutting back on your eating, trying to eliminate coffee or sugar, or simply trying to stop biting your finger-nails, all habits are hard to break! But the habit that is the most difficult to break, and that is the most harmful to your emotional state, is perhaps the habit that goes most unnoticed: the habit of thinking negatively. You can tie your hands behind your back to prevent yourself from biting your nails, you can isolate yourself from alcohol or cigarettes so that they are not available to you, you can withstand a few days of headaches and tiredness to get away from coffee, but you can never stop thinking!

As you have already seen, thinking is so natural to you that it's very easy to forget that you are doing it. When you start to recognize that you are actively thinking, you will be shocked at how often the content of your thinking is negative. I have been told by my own clients that once they started paying attention, they found that over 90 per cent of their thinking was in some way negative.

What Kind of Thinking is Negative?
This is a very important question because many people are so used to thinking negatively that they don't even

realize it's negative. Instead, they assume it's normal. The fact is, however, that any thinking that makes you feel less contented than before you started your train of thought can be considered negative. This includes, but is by no means limited to, thoughts related to how bad things are, the number of problems left unsolved, trying to figure out why something isn't right or why someone did something that hurt you or that doesn't meet with your approval, any kind of mental negative dialogue, and so on.

Most of us are used to reading, watching, or listening to the news reports of the day. Our thinking tends to mimic these reports. Our minds review past and future problems, our concerns and worries, and we speculate about how bad things really are. Obviously, some planning and review are needed for an effective life. If you are conscious of the fact that you are engaged in these mental activities, and you know the likely consequences of such mental activity, you are to a large degree protected from their negative effects. But if you engage yourself in these mental activities without realizing what you are doing to yourself, you are going to be at the mercy of your own thinking. Because this type of thinking is negative, your spirits will continue to drop or remain low. Once you understand and are able to witness this dynamic in action, you can then choose which trains of thought to follow and which ones to ignore. You will create a new habit of thinking only about those things that are truly useful and you will learn to ignore the others.

This type of selective thinking is not denial, nor is it apathy. Denial means pretending, and you are not pretending anything. You are acknowledging the problems in the world and the problems in your own life. You are simply choosing not to dwell on the negative thoughts you have about life because you know what will happen if you do.

Your experience of life is directly related to where you choose to focus your attention. If you focus on your thoughts of problems, your experience of life will consist mainly of problems. As you learn to move your focus of attention away from the problems and wrongs of the world and your life, you will find yourself noticing more beauty and kindness. This is exactly what small children do on a regular basis. They live in the same world that adults do, it's just that they notice different aspects of life. They see humour, compassion and opportunities.

You Can Choose Love Instead of Fear

As I explained in chapter 8, each time negative, pessimistic, or sceptical thoughts enter your mind, you are at a new choice point in your life. You can choose to follow your negative train of thought (your negative internal dialogue) as you have done in the past. This is the path that many people take, most of the time. It always seems like a reasonable thing to do because it happens so quickly and because it is so familiar to you. In fact, as you have already seen, rarely do you even know the internal dialogue is going on. An example of this would be the following. A series of thoughts enters your mind about how angry your parents (boss, children, spouse) are going to be with you because of something you have done. You play it out in your head and it makes you angry. In your mind, you start to justify your position to your parent (or whomever) and, again, you play it out to some conclusion. Of course, as you do this, you are feeling the negative effects of your thinking without even knowing that your thinking is causing you harm. The usual response to this self-induced pain is to blame your life and the people in it for the dissatisfaction you are feeling.

There is another way. Your choice point is that

moment when your internal dialogue began. You had a brief moment to decide, 'Do I follow this train of thought, or do I choose to stay in a feeling of love?'

What does it mean to 'choose love'? This means that you decide that feeling peace and contentment is more important to you than being right. It means instant resolution rather than ongoing struggle. It means feeling happy instead of feeling frustrated. Choosing to follow the path of love means you understand that the simple, peaceful feeling of your own healthy functioning is enough for you — it represents everything you ultimately want in your life. *Life doesn't get any better than the simple experience of your own mental health.* The only rationale for choosing to follow a negative train of thought would be some misconception on your part that doing so would bring you some sort of satisfaction. It won't! The satisfaction you are looking for is available to you only when you consciously decide that you want peace of mind at that moment and that you are willing to give up the thoughts that keep you from it. The only thing you have to do to discover your healthy functioning is to drop the thinking that is getting in the way.

Choosing love is not denial. What are you denying other than the source of your own pain? Nothing. You are consciously deciding *not* to feed the only fuel your pain has to eat. When you stop feeding your negative thinking, your emotional pain disappears, and with the disappearance comes a new feeling within you, the feeling of your healthy psychological functioning, the feeling of love. When you choose love instead of fear, you will stop fighting your own thinking and you will feel good again. Sometimes it will seem easier to follow your bad feelings than to find the good ones. Nevertheless, you can choose to look for, and stay with, the deeper, more positive feelings that exist within you.

This conscious choosing is very practical — but it isn't always easy. It doesn't just happen — you have to make it happen. You have to want it to happen more than you want to follow those seductive trains of thought that are so familiar to you. The good news is that this is all you have to do! Once you make this decision and make it a top priority in your life, the rest will fall into place.

One of the nice by-products of consciously choosing love instead of fear is that the recurring issues in your life begin to resolve themselves. Each time you have an opportunity to choose love instead of fear — and you make that choice — you are feeding a new kind of energy in your life, a positive and loving kind of energy.

Following every negative train of thought that enters your mind is the 'old' energy you are replacing. This old energy, filled with negativity, is what kept the issues in place for so long. How are you going to avoid having arguments with your parent, spouse, child, or boss if your mind is filled with negativity? You won't. Instead you will play out the problems and conflicts in your mind, then manifest them in your life. If you are like most people, you will be frustrated because the same things will keep happening to you. This is the cycle that needs to be broken. The way to break it is to see the choice points in your life and then follow the path towards your healthy functioning.

Janie was introduced to the concept of choice points the very first time she visited my office. Her husband was a workaholic who had little time or energy left for her. Janie was angry and resentful, and felt justified in her feelings. One of the first things she told me was, 'Anyone in my situation would be equally upset.'

Prior to coming to see me, Janie thought the best way to overcome her negative feelings was to talk to someone about them. Almost every day she would meet a friend for lunch to talk about her frustrations. And, like clockwork, every day she would finish lunch feeling resentful.

Janie discovered something surprising. The only times she was really upset about her husband were the times she was actively thinking about his long hours. She had assumed that she was *always* upset because whenever the issue came to her mind, it made her angry. For the most part, however, she was too involved in her own life to be concerned about her husband's schedule. She had a career of her own. She also enjoyed exercising at a health club as well as volunteering for a local organization. For the most part, while she was involved in her daily activities, she was quite content.

Janie learned that when thoughts of her husband's overworking came to her mind, she was at a very important choice point. One direction, thinking about his long hours and how work always came first, would take her straight towards her resentful feelings. The more resentful she felt, the more she would analyse how his schedule affected her life, which would send her into a tailspin of frustration. The other direction, the direction of warm loving feelings, would lead her straight towards gratitude. Taking this direction involved recognizing she was beginning to think negatively towards her husband, knowing what would happen if she were to continue, and choosing to drop her thoughts about the issue. She quickly learned that feeling warm towards her husband even in his absence, greatly improved the quality of her life.

Interestingly enough, Janie was able to take her understanding and implement it, not only during the day, but also when she was with her husband. She found that she appreciated the time she did have with him far more than she used to. Her husband responded beautifully to her warming feeling and the two of them are spending far more time together than they ever have. You have hundreds of choice points every day. In fact, you are at a choice point right now, this very moment, as you read this sentence. Do you follow your sceptical thoughts like, 'This can't work,' or do you use this choice point to your advantage, to grow and to change and to become happier? With intention, you can detect your own sceptical thoughts as they form, and simply drop them, coming back to your healthy functioning. This moment can be a new beginning for you. Choose the path of love instead of the path of fear and your life will begin to change right now!

How Can You Tell How Much of Your Own Thinking is Negative?

Start by sitting in a chair and closing your eyes. Clear your mind as much as you can. Sit quietly for a few minutes and simply pay attention to what comes to your mind.

Start paying attention to what you are thinking about during various times of the day — when you wake up, while you are eating, brushing your teeth, getting ready to go out, sitting alone, driving your car or riding on the bus, while you are walking, right now, and so on.

You are undoubtedly going to be surprised at how often some form of negativity comes to your mind. You will probably think of problems, concerns, things that need to be done that you really don't want to do, things that might happen, things that might not happen, things that shouldn't happen, things what did happen that you wish hadn't happened, things you should have said, wanted to say, didn't want to say, things that other people said that bothered you, things that other people did that bothered you, people who didn't act as you thought they should, and on and on and on!

As you begin to take note of what you think about

all day long, please be easy on yourself. As I said, thinking in this way is a habit. Like all habits, it wasn't formed overnight. It took years to develop and it may take a little time to break.

I am not suggesting that it's never appropriate to think negatively or that it's never OK to whine or complain — you certainly have that right, and a little isn't going to kill you. What I am suggesting is that most people — probably yourself included — spend an exorbitant amount of time engaged in negative thinking without even realizing it. You have a great deal of internal dialogue going on in your mind that doesn't seem like anything at all because you are so accustomed to it — and for this reason it's hard to stop. Also, it's human nature to want to improve your life. As long as your life isn't perfect, your analytical mind and your ego will always be searching for ways that you can improve. Your thinking mind will constantly remind you that you aren't good enough. No matter how hard you try, your ego will never be satisfied with what you come up with.

Obviously, the circumstances in your life will never be perfect, so if you believe that thinking about ways to improve your life is a good deal, you will spend the rest of your life doing so. Many people follow this path. They have conversations within their own heads that seem, on the surface, to be resolving various issues, while in reality nothing changes.

If you can become conscious of the fact that you engage in this negative internal dialogue, and you can wake up to the fact that you are doing it while you are doing it, and you know that you are harming yourself, you will be protected. This is a very powerful secret to becoming a happier person. I have worked with hundreds of happy people. Every single one of them agrees that becoming aware of and learning to turn off their internal dialogue was a major factor in their development into happy people. Don't allow your own internal dialogue to run (and ruin) your life. Turn it off, or at least redirect it along a more positive route. Remind yourself frequently to drop your negative thinking. When negative thoughts fill your head, let them go. Allow them to drift away knowing they aren't important. Don't focus on them — say to yourself, 'it's not worth it.' Rest assured that your internal dialogue is hurting no one except yourself. Once you understand the root cause of your negative feelings — where they come from and what holds them in place — and make the commitment to catch yourself in the act, the rest will fall into place. You will learn to tap into a nicer feeling within yourself which will make your life run smoothly. As your mind quietens down, the panic and hurry will fade away. Answers that you have always searched for will be as prevalent as the questions used to be.

To free yourself from unhappiness you *must* understand that your negative thinking — nothing else — is the cause of your negative feelings. Without the negative thoughts there would be nothing to make you feel bad.

Now, this very instant, stop reading and take notice of how you are feeling! Just pause for a minute and see how you are feeling. If your mind is quieter than it usually is, notice the quiet. Notice how good it feels. OK, now read on.

Did you notice a difference in how you felt? Did you notice your mind to be a little quieter? If you did, you were tapping into your own healthy functioning. Or did you think to yourself, as you read the last sentence, something like 'It's more complicated than that'? If you did, remember it was that thought and nothing else that made you feel less than OK. If you hadn't had that thought you would be feeling different right now. If you understand what you are reading, you will be able to start catching yourself thinking your way into an unhappy or depressed state. The very first time you notice the thoughts that are pulling you away from your healthy functioning, and you let them go instead of focusing on them, you will notice the quieter feeling within you. You will be on your way to a life without depression. You'll see how much power you have over the way you feel. You'll feel the power of your own healthy functioning.

Some of the mental processes that you have been engaging in, prior to now, can be described as well-practised mental mistakes. If you stop engaging in these processes you can open the door to a new feeling of contentment. This new feeling is the one you have been looking and hoping for. You can access this feeling by letting go of the thoughts that are interfering with or covering up your healthy functioning.

Even if you understand and agree with what you are reading, you will still have difficulty breaking the habit of negative thinking. The reason, again, is that you are so used to thinking in certain ways that you won't even realize you are thinking negatively. Your thinking happens so automatically that it's going to take some time to create a new habit of *not* thinking negatively.

The Accumulation Factor

It's easy to allow yourself to become discouraged or sceptical if you don't notice an instant connection between what you are thinking and how you are feeling — for example, if you say to yourself, 'I am happy,' then immediately after that you say to yourself, 'There, I had a positive thought. Now why don't I feel happy?'

Two factors explain why you don't always feel an immediate corresponding positive emotion to every positive thought. First, take a look at the thought that followed the positive thought: immediately after your positive thought you had a sceptical thought. Here is your habit coming into play. You give yourself plenty of time for negativity, on and off throughout the day, but once you have a positive thought, you immediately sabotage it with a negative one. It's tricky because it all happens so quickly. It's important to realize that if you didn't have the negativity after the positive thinking you would feel good.

The second factor that prevents you from feeling good immediately after you think positively is equally important. I call this the 'accumulation factor'. It suggests that you accumulate negativity in your mind throughout the day, and throughout your lifetime. Because of the vast negativity that has accumulated in your mind, eventually you have a negative thought that 'breaks the camel's back'. It's not any one thought that does you in, it's the accumulation that builds up over time.

If you were to eliminate 90 to 95 per cent of the useless accumulation of negative thoughts that you have, the same thoughts that now send you spinning into a depressed state would have little, if any, impact on you. Almost no single thought is going to have that much power over you, but with hundreds, or even thousands, of accumulated negative thoughts passing through your mind, it's just a matter of time before you can't handle them any longer and unhappiness or depression sets in. Set a goal for yourself of eliminating as close to 100 per cent of your daily negativity as possible. The closer you get to reaching this goal, the less impact each individual negative thought is going to have on your emotional well-being.

Sometimes it can be helpful, especially at first, if you keep a log of your progress. Obviously you will never catch yourself all the time you are thinking negatively, because, as you have seen, the problem is that most of your negativity goes unnoticed. Keeping a log, however, can help you stay focused on your goal. You can keep the log very general. For example, you might make very general insertions three times a day, something like: 'This morning I stayed away from negativity very well.' Then after lunch you might insert, 'Be careful, I was getting carried away again,' and so forth. A log can serve as a constant reminder of what you are trying to do. It can keep your 'accumulated totals' to a minimum.

How Do I Break My Habit of Negative Thinking?

There are two ways that I know of to ensure that you break your habit of negative thinking. The first is to tell a friend, or even a paid consultant, to monitor what you say for at least two days. Ask him or her to interpret and stop you every time you fall into your old pattern. Tell him that you don't want him to let you say anything negative or self-defeating; no 'I have a right to be upset,' no 'You'll never guess what happened to me today' (if it was bad), no 'I never should have done that,' or any of the literally thousands of other self-defeating possibilities. You can't afford to be too selective in what you cut out, especially at first. The best way to eliminate the negative thinking in your life is to strive to eliminate it altogether. The idea here is to break the old habit of negative thinking and replace it with a new habit of ignoring your negative thinking. You may be very surprised at how often you will be interrupted. Don't take it personally and try to maintain a sense of humour about it. Your friend or consultant is there only to help you. Once you break the habit, you can go back to your normal life and things will be different. You will still engage your mind in negativity from time to time, but your experience of the negativity will be very different.

Believe it or not, it will seem worse. That's right, worse. In fact, once your own negative thinking seems worse than it used to, you're on your way to recovery, because you will have transformed a habit. Something that you have always assumed was perfectly normal, necessary, and healthy will now sound like a herd of buffalo running through your head. You will *feel* the difference. As your own negative thinking begins to sound loud and obnoxious, you will be less and less interested in continuing. The result is that you will begin to turn off the thinking you took for granted for so long. As I said earlier, avoiding focusing on your negative thinking is not denial. It's smart! You aren't denying that you are having the thoughts, you are simply training your mind to ignore what you don't want. As less and less energy is spent on negative thoughts, you will find that there are fewer and fewer negative thoughts demanding your attention.

The second way to break the habit of negative thinking is perhaps even simpler, but will take more discipline on your part. You will have to do this one by yourself. You will need a large index card on which you should write 'What am I thinking now?' Write these words in big, bold letters and carry the card with you everywhere you go for at least one month. As often as possible, every few minutes if you can, look at the card. I know it sounds tedious and even childish — in some ways it is — but *it works!* You will start to see how often you sabotage yourself with negativity, and you will be able to stop doing it. The idea behind both of these exercises is identical. You are attempting to break an old habit — that doesn't seem like a habit. Negative thinking may seem normal to most people, but it doesn't have to be for you.

What Do I Think Instead?
Many people are frightened of what will happen if they stop thinking negatively, because they are used to it.

What will you think instead? The answer to this question is very simple: it doesn't matter. This is not a glib answer. As you catch yourself thinking negatively, and consciously set out to stop doing it, you will find that your mind will be much clearer and freer than it ever has been before. More creative thoughts will naturally replace the old ones. You will be a much more dynamic person. You will seem fresh and new, inspired and uplifted. The last thing in the world you will have to worry about is not having enough to think about!

The only word to describe what will happen to you if you stop thinking negatively is *amazing*. In the absence of negative thinking you will feel like a new person. Your healthy functioning will take over your life. Your thoughts will be different, your attitude will be different, and most of all, the way you feel will be different. You will feel good again. There is simply no way to feel bad if you aren't thinking bad and if you are in control of what you are thinking.

Before you go on reading, try it right now. Let your thoughts flow. If any form of negativity enters your mind, let it pass by. Don't give it the time of day. Remain uninterested in the negativity. Put your attention on your healthy functioning. How are you feeling?

The answer to this question is entirely dependent on the way you are thinking. If you are thinking hopeful and positive thoughts, that is the way you will be feeling; if you are thinking negative, pessimistic thoughts, you will be feeling that way.

The bottom line is this: you become what you think about all day long. Do you want to think about misery, pain, and problems, or do you want to think about love, kindness, hope, and potential? The answer to this question will, to a large extent, determine how you are going to feel. Give it a try. It can work for you. You can feel good again!

Moods

One of the most undeniable facts about human beings is that each of us has what are referred to as 'moods.' There has never been, nor will there ever be, a person who doesn't experience the ups and downs of moods. Even the happiest person isn't immune to them. Your moods greatly affect your awareness of the fact that you are potentially hurting yourself with your own thinking. Your mood level also affects what you think about, as well as your ability to realize that you are at a choice point. Understanding the nature and the deceptive power of your moods will help you ease rather than fight your way out of an unhappy state of mind.

Moods are like the tides of the sea. They are constantly changing and shifting. Sometimes moods are very high, sometimes they are very low, and sometimes they are somewhere in between. And although it may not seem like it when you are feeling low, your moods are *always* changing, although perhaps only a little at a time.

Even if you have been depressed for a long time, you can probably remember what a good mood feels like. If you can't remember, here is a reminder: in high moods life feels good and happy, light-hearted, easy, fun, rewarding, simple and care-free. In high moods you experience your greatest wisdom and common sense, and you can solve problems and make decisions in a relaxed fashion. When you are in a high mood you have a sense of gratitude for your life, you appreciate the people close to you, you are easily satisfied, and you don't take things personally.

When you are in a low mood life appears to be just the opposite. Everything seems very serious and difficult. The slightest annoyance causes great frustration. In low moods we lose virtually all of our common sense. We take things personally and there is a underlying sense of urgency and despair.

Your experience in a low mood is exactly the same as your experience in a depression. In fact, except for the duration of the mood, the two are essentially identical. Depression is nothing more than a prolonged and painful low mood.

An extremely important question to ponder is why do moods come and go for most people, while they hang on in the form of a negative feeling state or depression for others? The answer is that some people have certain mental habits that they tend to practise in low moods, without realizing that they are exercising them, or that they are causing any problems. Unfortunately, if you perpetuate these processes while you are in a low mood, you will remain low.

To escape a negative state of mind, you must begin to recognize when you are in a low mood and to avoid the processes that will keep you there. If you learn to do this, you will find yourself going up and down like everyone else, rather than remaining down in the dumps.

What Happens to Your Thinking When You Are in a Low Mood?

The quality of your thinking suffers greatly when you are in a low mood. When you feel bad, it is absolutely predictable that you will think in a negative way. The lower your mood, the more intense will be your negative thoughts. The thoughts you have about your life when you are experiencing a low mood will be very different from the thoughts you will have when you are experiencing a higher mood. Perhaps the easiest way to understand this idea is to compare the following two conversations I had with the same person. These conversations were taped on two consecutive days with a client in my stress-management practice. (He knew he was being taped.)

Day 1 – Low Mood Thinking
Therapist: 'How are you?'
Client: 'Terrible, almost unbearable.'
Therapist: 'I read in the business section of the paper that your company was doing quite well.'
Client: 'You'd never know it the way they treat us. There's no job security anyway. I hate my job.'
Therapist: 'Didn't you used to like your job?'
Client: 'Not that I remember. How could I, anyway?'

Day 2 – Higher Mood Thinking
Therapist: 'How are you?'
Client: 'Fine, how are you?'
Therapist: 'Great, thanks. My wife is expecting another baby soon. We're really excited.'
Client: 'That's nice, I really like babies.'
Therapist: 'By the way, I saw another article in the paper today about your company. Seems they are donating some money to the hungry this holiday season.'
Client: 'Yeah, I'm a part of that programme. We're diverting a small percentage of pre-tax profit to a local social-services agency.'
Therapist: 'Sounds rewarding.'
Client: 'Yeah, it is.'

This is an example of the power of moods. Believe it or not, these types of conversations are very common, not just in a professional setting, but in everyday life. Doesn't it seem as if entirely different people are talking? It's because this person is seeing and experiencing life differently in different moods. In low moods, your own thinking is always dark and pessimistic. If you look into your past when you are low you will see a painful past, your life will seem to have been a waste. If you look towards the future, your life will appear hopeless. Interestingly, however, when you look to your past when your mood is higher, it appears far happier than it did in a lower mood. The same is true with regard to your future. The higher the mood, the more hopeful it appears.

The reason I taped my client's conversations was to show him the delusionary quality of his own moods, to show him firsthand how his low moods distort his vision of life. In terms of escaping unhappiness, the important point here is simple: the negative thoughts that fill your mind in a low mood are *the cause* of your suffering — and those thoughts almost always contain gross distortions. Although the thoughts you have while in a low mood *seem* valid to you, they aren't. They are almost always irrational and distorted. When you start to see the inevitability of negative thinking when you feel bad, you can begin to distrust and ignore what you are thinking in the same way that you would ignore a mirage in a desert. When my client listened to his own voice it became very obvious to him: 'Wow,' he said, in a somewhat shocked tone. 'I can't believe that was me.' Far more important, however, was the fact that he could now see, for the first time, that his thinking in his low moods was and always had been 'pathetic' (his word). He realized that to believe his own thinking when he was in a low state was 'crazy', a self-written prescription for pain and suffering. When he is low, he simply can't see life clearly. His vision of life is distorted, and he's far better off clearing his mind and turning off his thinking.

What makes understanding moods so difficult is that every time you are low, you will feel justified and certain that the way you are feeling is appropriate and necessary. You will feel a sense of urgency and self-righteousness and you will want so badly to believe in what you are thinking. The only way out is to see the absolute absurdity of believing in what you are thinking and feeling when you are low, and then making a commitment to yourself to ignore your own thoughts whenever you find yourself in such a state. You must understand that your thoughts, in a low feeling state, are not worth paying attention to. They can only hurt you since they contain only gross distortions. Once you are convinced of this, you will see the application to your life. You will know that life will always look better later if you let it alone, for now.

If you are unconvinced, start keeping track of the people you know. Ask them questions when they are low and keep track of their answers. See how well they solve problems, how clearly they think, how much sense they make, and how much love and appreciation they have for their family and friends. Then compare their low-mood living to their high-mood living. The next time they are feeling better, even if it's only a little better, ask them the same questions. What you will discover may be shocking to you. You will see that you have two different friends — Dr Jekyll and Mr Hyde!

The reason it may not have seemed possible to escape unhappiness until now is that you haven't understood the origin and cause of unhappiness. Without understanding the cause, it's likely that you have been engaging in activities that have added fuel to the fire —

primarily low-mood thinking and lots of it.

One of the major problems with low moods is that they always seem as though they will last forever. It's a lot like being in a dark cave and not being able to see any light — it's frightening. If you have been in a particular cave, however, five hundred times, even though you can't see the light, you know that it is there, and you will have no reason to panic. You know that it's just a matter of time before you find the light.

The process of waiting out a low mood is no different from trying to find your way out of a cave. No matter how many times you've been there before, it seems that this is the worst one ever and that you are justified in being upset. It always *seems* that this one will last forever. But it won't. If you know what's happening while it's happening, you are protected from the effects of your mood. There's nothing to fear. The light is just around the corner as long as you don't panic and as long as you walk in the right direction. Having faith that your low mood will lift is like having faith that the trick mirror you are looking into at the amusement park isn't giving you a clear vision of reality. Both are illusions. Once you know that what you are feeling is nothing more than an illusion, you won't let your mind spiral you further into unhappiness.

Low moods really aren't a problem in and of themselves. Of course they're difficult, and no one likes them, but they can't harm you if you know what's going on. The real problem is the thinking and the mental activity that accompany the low mood. When you are in a low mood, your thoughts are going to be negative, insecure, and pessimistic. Your life and everything in it will look bad. You will always be able to come up with many reasons why you feel so bad and theories to support and justify your misery. No matter what you come up with, regardless of how accurate you are, or how bad things look, it can only hurt you. Why? Because the reasons themselves (the thinking about it) fuel the low mood. Without the reason, the mood would pass on its own. Once you introduce a reason, however, your low mood can't pass, because you have injected fuel to keep it going. The more you think about it, the worse it will seem.

Ignoring the negative thoughts you have while you are in a low mood is not denial, nor is it dangerous or irresponsible. Your problems, if they are real, will still be there when your mood goes up. The only difference will be that you will be more equipped to solve them. When you are low, what kinds of answers do you realistically think you will come up with? Futile answers, I can assure you.

Even after you learn this approach to escaping unhappiness, you will still be at risk of being negatively affected by your low moods. The reason is that when you drop into a low mood all you will see are problems. And you can get pretty clever at justifying to yourself why this low mood is different from the last one or the tens of thousands that preceded it. The more you entertain the reasons you come up with, and the thoughts you are having about your predicament, the worse you will feel — every single time. Your protection will be, however, that you will no longer trust what you are feeling when you are low. You will usually know that you're being tricked by your own low mood. You will usually know that even though it's tempting to indulge your negative thoughts, if you don't, you'll be far better off. Your protection will be that you will usually know that your distressed feelings will pass if you can somehow just leave them alone. You will usually know that, even though your reasons for your unhappiness seem to be good ones, the reasons themselves are a big part of the problem.

I say 'usually' when I refer to your new protection because everyone gets tricked some of the time. No matter how conscious you become of the process, you will still take the bait once in a while. Even when you do take it, however, the effects won't last nearly as long. Your recovery will be much quicker.

If Thinking Keeps You Down, What Brings Your Mood Back Up?

If you don't interfere with the natural rhythm of your moods, they will go up and down all by themselves. This was true for people in the tenth century and it will be true for people in the twenty-second century. Moods are a constant, they are a fact of life, as is their changeability.

Even happy people have their own share of downs. One of the differences, however, between a depressed person and a non-depressed person, is that a non-depressed person accepts that she has moods. She makes allowances for this in her attitude and in her behaviour. She says things like, 'Things don't look so good right now. Ask me later,' or 'I'm in a really bad mood right now. Don't bother me.' She knows it is a temporary problem — it feels bad and it's no fun, but it will pass if she lets it be. The tide will return.

Depressed people also have low moods and those moods also feel terrible. The saving grace, however, that depressed people often don't realize is that their mood isn't permanent. Depressed people describe their low mood differently from non-depressed people. Instead of saying, 'Things don't look so good right now. Ask me later,' a depressed person might say, 'Don't ask me. I'm depressed.' There is an *assumed* sense of permanency that in actuality doesn't have to exist.

It's your understanding that moods are a natural fact of life that will bring you out of a low mood. Accepting the fact that you are low, but at the same time realizing that your mood will rise on its own, allows the darkness to lift. The truth is, *you don't have to do anything.* In fact, the less you do the better off you'll be. Your mood *will* begin to lift as you stop paying attention to all that you think about when you are low, and you begin to ignore the thoughts and feelings you are having. Don't make the mistake of believing you will become apathetic if you implement this understanding in your life. Far from it. As your mood lifts, you will become far more immersed and more present in your life. Any real problems you may have will most certainly still be there, but you will be far more equipped to deal with them. You are not ignoring your life or your problems, you are simply ignoring your distorted thinking.

Ellen and Stan have been running a small business together for almost a year. Business has been pretty good and the two of them, who started out as friends, have been working together very nicely.

One day, out of the blue, Ellen comes to the office in a terrible mood. Ellen's way to act out her low mood (everyone does it differently) is to become very critical. She immediately begins pointing out all of Stan's imperfections and all the ways he could be doing better. Stan is amazed; he's never seen this side of Ellen before.

Stan knows little about the power of moods and takes Ellen's comments personally. He becomes frightened and insecure because he fears he has seen 'the real Ellen'. His mood begins to drop dramatically. Stan's way of acting out a low mood is to become defensive and argumentative, which fuels Ellen's criticism, frightens her, and lowers her mood even further.

In a low mood, every little thing can look like 'the tip of the iceberg'. Both Stan and Ellen begin to wonder if they should shut down the business. They fear that this is just the beginning of a series of new problems. Since neither Stan nor Ellen understands moods, they believe the thoughts they are having about each other. The way they feel, of course, dictates the way they treat each other. Their business begins to suffer.

When Stan and Ellen came to see me they were frustrated. Both were surprised when I didn't analyse or even discuss their patterns of criticism and defensiveness. I talked to them about how they had innocently brought out the very worst in each other by taking each other's low-mood reactions too seriously. I taught them to expect negative behaviour from their partner when they fell into a very low mood and to make allowances in their own mind for such behaviour. I also taught them to be compassionate towards themselves and not to take themselves as seriously when they were trapped in low moods.

This wasn't a miracle cure or an extraordinary case. It was simply two people who had become blinded by their own low moods. Once they understood the nature of moods, they let go of their frustration and went on with their lives.

◈11◈

Living in the Present Moment

Perhaps the oldest and wisest piece of advice for escaping depression and living a happier life is to live in the present moment. Virtually every spiritual teacher and wise person throughout history has suggested this solution. And although many of us have heard this age-old advice, and have even agreed with it, the question remains: why is it so difficult? The answers to this question are surprisingly simple. There are two factors that keep people tied to their past and speculating about a negative future, both of which we have already discussed: very few people have the necessary under-standing of their own thinking, and very few people understand the power of their own moods.

If you believe that your thinking is something that happens to you — instead of something that you are doing to create an experience of life — it is *impossible* for you to live in the present moment. If you feel, for whatever reason, that you must follow trains of thought as they enter your mind, you will be unable to remain in the present. Let's suppose you are all alone reading a book when suddenly a thought crosses your mind, 'I'll never be able to . . .' (and you fill in the blank). It could be any thought at all, it really doesn't matter. If you follow that train of thought, where do you suppose it's going to take you? Straight to the emotional dump! If you see, however, that all that has occurred has been a thought racing through your head — a simple and harmless thought which you choose to dismiss — you will be free from its effects.

Please don't assume that this is too simplistic to be true. It's not! Let's look at it logically. One second prior to the thought entering your mind you were busy reading a book. Then, from out of nowhere, a thought pops into your head. What makes you take it seriously, follow it, and become upset or immobilized by it except habit? The problem has been that no one has ever assured you, until now, that you don't need to be frightened or upset by your own thoughts. Would you have been upset if the thought that entered your mind was instead 'I love my cat'? Of course not! You don't need to be upset by either thought because both are just thoughts. Once you understand the nature of your own thinking, the fact that you are the one manufacturing your own thoughts, and the fact that your thoughts are just thoughts and that they are harmless, you will have created the necessary emotional distance from your thinking to keep your attention on the here and now, the present moment.

If you feel the need to follow every train of thought that happens to enter your mind, you will be too busy elsewhere (in the past or in the future) to remain in the present moment; you will be too busy chasing and studying the various forms of negativity that enter your mind. There will be too much activity going on in your mind for you to control its contents, since somewhere in the region of fifty thousand thoughts will pass through your mind each day! If you believe that your thinking is caused by other people and the events going on around you, it's easy to see why your thinking can become overwhelming. As your understanding of thought deepens, however, and as you begin to see yourself as the creator of your own thoughts, and as you see your thoughts as something that can't harm you, you can step back from your own thinking, almost as though you were watching a movie instead of actually being in it. Then, if a frightening, depressing, angry or jealous thought enters your mind, you have the option to follow that thought and see where it takes you, or you can simply dismiss the thought and bring your attention back to whatever you are doing.

The second significant reason why people find it so difficult to remain in the present moment is that they don't understand the power of their own moods, and how to respond when their mood is low. Unfortunately, if you believe in what you think when you are low, you will be too frightened to remain in the present moment. Remember, low moods will always promote negative, pessimistic thinking, and in your low moods you will feel a tremendous sense of urgency — a feeling that you need to do something to get away from the way you feel. In low moods, insecure thoughts will dominate your consciousness. The very best you can do is to distrust, dismiss, and ignore your thoughts when you are low. You must understand that life will *always* look serious, urgent, and problematic when you are down. You have to expect this to be the case and be prepared in advance. You must also remember that life always looks better when your spirits lift, even if they lift only a little.

If you don't distrust your thinking when you are in a low mood, your head will be full of imagined gloom and doom. Your problems will seem too urgent to remain in the here and now and you will feel as though you need to speculate as to how you are going to escape the way you feel.

Happy people know deep within themselves that regardless of what happened yesterday, a month ago, or in their early childhood, and what may or may not happen tomorrow, next week, or in 15 years, the 'now' is where they will find their happiness — and the 'now' is where depression cannot exist.

A genuinely happy person knows that life is nothing more than a constant series of present moments to be experienced, one right after another. He sees the past for what it was able to teach him about how to live more in the 'now' and the future as more present moments to be experienced when they eventually arrive. Happy people strive to be fully with the person they are with, to be involved with whatever they are doing without thinking too much about the future or the past. They strive to experience each present moment of their lives to its fullest. A happy person knows that the closer he gets to his goal of living each day in the present, the more he guarantees a wonderful experience of life. Living in the present is not a theory; it is the reality that a happy person lives in.

Many clients have reported to me that the time they feel most immersed in the present moment is when they are either playing with or watching children. Perhaps the best way to describe the difference between present-moment living and non-present-moment living is this: present-moment living means you are choosing to focus your attention on what is happening right now; you enjoy and appreciate just this moment. You know that you have no time to lose — your life is too important — and there is no better time to live and appreciate your life than right now. You feel terrific because you aren't speculating about your life, you are living your life. You are not thinking about what's next until it's time to do so. Non-present-moment living can be described this way: instead of living in the moment, you are waiting for the next one. Instead of enjoying where you are, you are concerned about what might be. Instead of immersing yourself in this moment, you are speculating about the future or rehashing the past.

Noticing how good it feels to live in the present moment with my children has helped me to realize that whenever I am not feeling good I have slipped out of the present moment. You can have the same realization in your life by noticing how removed from the present you are when you aren't feeling well. The next time you feel depressed, notice where your thoughts are. I guarantee that they will be somewhere other than right where you are. Once you feel the connection between the present moment and your healthy functioning you will know that the solution to your depression lies in your ability to bring your attention back to the present moment.

Children are the best examples of people who fully absorb themselves in the present moment. A client of mine who works with pre-school children describes it this way: 'They allow themselves to stay completely involved in whatever they happen to be doing and with whomever they happen to be with. Because children are so in the moment, they milk every ounce out of their experience.'

As an adult, you may have got into the habit of allowing past regrets and future concerns to squeeze the life out of your present moments. As you become conscious of how you sabotage your life by your thoughts of the past and the future you can begin dropping those thoughts and noticing a happier feeling returning within yourself.

As you become more orientated to the present moment, you will open the door to enjoying your life. Instead of seeing potential problems, you will see beauty; instead of reviewing past mistakes, you will learn from your mistakes and move forward. When negative or insecure thoughts enter your mind, you will see them the same way you would see ants at a picnic — distractions that can be ignored. You would certainly prefer the ants not to be at your picnic, but you wouldn't let them ruin an otherwise perfectly beautiful day. I have the same feeling about negative thoughts that enter my mind every single day. I often wish they would leave me alone, but I refuse to let them drain enjoyment from my life. Instead of harping on my negative thoughts, I feel grateful that I am able to dismiss them. You, too, can dismiss any thoughts you have that you don't like. Remember, happy people have the same kinds of negative thoughts as do depressed people. The only difference is in the relationship between the thoughts and the thinker: happy people are able to see their thoughts as thoughts and dismiss the ones they don't want.

Someday Won't Be Different
One of the problems with living in the past or future is that thinking in these terms will never produce a happy life. A mind that believes it will be happy only when certain conditions are met will *always* create new conditions to satisfy once the old ones are completed. A cycle of 'I'll be happy when . . .' is created. The particulars can be virtually anything: 'When school is complete,' 'I get a job,' 'I get a promotion,' 'I make more money,' 'I find a mate,' 'I have a child,' 'I buy a home,' 'I solve these problems,' and so forth. Please don't misunderstand what I'm saying: these goals are not bad ideas in themselves. If you want a child or to make more money, or anything else, then do it! But future-orientated thinking will *guarantee* that you will not enjoy the process of achieving these goals and it will guarantee that you will not enjoy the results once you get them. Your mind will start again and you'll be in the same place you are right now.

If you want 'someday' to be different, you must make a personal commitment to begin to enjoy your life today, as it is right now. There is no other way. You are here anyway, so you might as well immerse yourself in the present moment and enjoy it. From now on, whenever you feel discouraged, angry, or in any way frustrated, try to notice how distant you are from this moment. You will find the same thing that I find when I feel less than happy — your mind will be producing thoughts that are reminding you about something in your past or something in your future. If you bring your attention back to this moment you will very quickly regain a more positive feeling and get on with your life. As your understanding of thought deepens, this will become easier and easier and your depression will disappear.

The point is obvious, but extremely important. The only genuine and lasting happiness you will ever find is right where you are. The present moment is a magical, ever-changing place that is waiting to be enjoyed. The present moment is a place where you are uniquely capable of such wonderment that it is impossible to experience anything other than happiness. Make a commitment today to pull in the reins of your thinking and start enjoying your life.

Eliminating Hurry

One of the secrets of living a life free of depression is to eliminate the sense of hurry in your life. Hurry is nothing more than a bad habit; it's not a scheduling problem, it's a state-of-mind problem. There are many extremely busy individuals who almost never feel hurried and even more people who really aren't very busy, but who feel busy almost all the time.

The degree to which you feel hurried in your life is dependent entirely on your ability to keep your attention in the present moment. Can you imagine what it would be like if all of your thoughts centred around what you have to do and how little time you have to do it? Pretty scary isn't it? To one degree or another, many of us do the very same thing. We fill up our present moments with thoughts of a hurried future.

The solution of all hurry is to live more in the present moment. In fact, it is impossible to feel hurried regardless of what you are doing when you become less consumed with what needs to be done, and more consumed with using each moment to its fullest.

If you are running late and driving to your next appointment, letting your head spin forwards in time to all the terrible things that are going to happen once you arrive isn't going to get you there one second quicker. If you can learn to bring your attention back to the moment — to simply driving the car — you will find that you will arrive in a much better emotional condition. Instead of feeling frazzled and irritated, you will feel confident and friendly. If you are late, you will be able to explain and apologize to the person you are with and then both of you can get on with your agenda.

A happy person knows that as long as he continues thinking about things yet to be done he will continue to feel hurried — it's that simple. He knows that a hurried mind cannot be a happy one because a hurried mind is consumed not with involvement and joy but with future activities that are yet to be experienced. Happy people know that their minds are capable of making them feel hurried even when they're not under a time pressure. Luckily, they also know that they are capable of bringing their attention back to this moment, and back to whatever they are doing.

Certainly there will be times when you need to do things quickly or take immediate action, but from this moment on, do yourself a favour and save your sense of hurry for those special and rare occasions when it's truly necessary. One of the most eye-opening experiences in life is simply to notice how often you rush around unnecessarily. Once you notice this tendency, you can eliminate most of it by simply bringing yourself back to right here where you are now. As you become a witness to your own heightened pace, you can step back from it and slow down. Try it today and I'm sure you'll find that it's much easier than it sounds. Once you train your mind to be right here, and to enjoy or fully utilize this moment — one moment at a time — you will start ignoring your more hurried thoughts when they do enter your mind.

Life isn't an Emergency

Life can be an enormously rewarding experience; a totally fulfilling and creative experience where virtually every activity is seen as yet another wonderful opportunity. Although it's often treated as one, life is not an emergency; it's not meant to be constantly postponed while we anxiously rush around and attempt to 'get everything done'.

Life is meant to be lived, one moment at a time. Whether you are 18 years old or 80 years old, male or female, dark or light, rich or poor, you are given the same gift and it's administered in exactly the same way. The gift is life itself and it's given to us one precious moment at a time. Life isn't an emergency, it's an adventure. Once you commit yourself to seeing life this way you will be amazed at how quickly your life will change for the better. You will notice the beauty instead of the ugliness, the caring instead of the non-caring, and the grace instead of the misfortune. Remember, life isn't an emergency.

Don't Postpone All of Your Gratification

The 'someday life will be better' philosophy of living leaves an awful lot to be desired. For one thing, it's simply not true. If you are still thinking in future terms when 'someday' does arrive, you will still be unhappy. Future-orientated thinking will always leave you disappointed and frustrated because you never quite immerse yourself in the now; you're never practised enjoying the reward so you never know what to do with it when it arrives. It's almost as though future-oriented thinking is one step removed from life: 'I'll love my life when I get a job.' When you get the job, however, you are so accustomed to thinking in non-present terms that your mind will do it all over again: 'I can't be happy now because I have to start at the bottom of the ladder, but I will be happy when I get more responsibility.' This endless cycle must be broken to free yourself of depression.

Don't postpone all of your gratification, or even most of it. It's not worth it and you don't have to. Live as much of your life as you can *right now*. You will find your greatest pleasure right here, in this moment. Whatever you happen to be doing, do it as well as you can. Five minutes from now, do the same thing; an hour from now do the same thing again; tomorrow, the same thing. Strive to enjoy thoroughly each step of your activities and goals. If you do, then once you achieve your goal you will enjoy your success as well.

Let me make one thing clear. People who live for the now are not sacrificing future plans or success, not one bit! On the contrary, a person who is immersed in the present is doing the best possible job that can be done. If you look at the greatest athletes you'll watch how totally absorbed in the present day they are, and that is the secret of their success.

Problems Will Disappear

As you live your life increasingly in the present moment you will notice that your problems will almost magically disappear. Because you are always doing the best you can when you focus on the now, your moments begin to blend together into natural solutions. Rather than spending your life worrying about what might happen, you are spending each moment constructively or enjoyably; each moment becomes another piece of the puzzle that is necessary to complete the whole.

Just as goals can only be achieved one step at a time, so too can problems only be solved by doing what you can, one step at a time, continually, moment to moment and day to day. I'm sure that you can see the logic in such thinking. As your attention focuses on the moment, on what can be done, instead of on the problem or on how difficult something is, you are marching towards solutions. Present-moment thinking focuses on what can be done right now to improve a situation. The action taken in this moment will lead to other solution- orientated actions as they are needed. As you do what you can, moment to moment, each of your problems that once seemed so insurmountable will fade away. Then you can get on with the business of living; your life will be more about living and less about solving problems. You will see that all worry is a waste of time and energy!

Live Each Day as If It Were Your Last

Happy people know that there are no guarantees on the duration of this adventure called life. They also know that this goes for everyone else. Reminding themselves of this simple truth helps them live every day of their lives as if it were their last — and who knows? It might be.

Happy people don't wait until tomorrow to let the

people that they love know that they love them; they don't postpone until tomorrow watching a beautiful sunset, visiting the countryside, or playing with their children. And happy people enjoy whatever they happen to be doing. If they are making sales calls to prospective clients, they vow to themselves to enjoy talking to each person, even if what they are doing happens to be called work. What difference does it really make? If you are absorbed in the moment, you can make that moment a rich experience.

If you knew you were never going to see your child or your spouse again, wouldn't you take an extra minute to give them a hug before running out of the door? Wouldn't you be more patient, kind, and understanding? Of course you would.

If you live each day as if it were your last, then when your last day arrives you will have no regrets. Your life will have been a masterpiece; you will have lived life the best way it can be lived — one moment at a time with grace and appreciation.

Forgiveness

Forgiveness stems from present-moment thinking. When you forgive someone, including yourself, you are saying to yourself, 'The past is over.' No one, not even yourself, can undo what is done. When you refuse to forgive someone you are *not* living in the present moment. You are hanging on to a past that no longer exists. You are torturing yourself with your own thinking.

Present-moment thinking allows you to forgive anyone and everyone, which frees you once and for all to enjoy your life as you deserve to do. If your past was painful, a lack of forgiveness only makes your present equally painful. No matter what happened to you, no matter how awful it was, the way to be happy now is to forgive anyone and everyone by living more in the present moment.

Life is What's Happening While You're Busy Making Other Plans

It's so tempting to fall into the habit of continually postponing your life until later. It's easy to believe, as so many people do, that life is going to get better and more rewarding at some later date. When you delve into the logic of such thinking, however, you will see that this is a tragic mistake.

When tomorrow arrives it will still be a series of present moments to be experienced. It's important to know that present-moment living does take practice and is not necessarily easy. Without a firm commitment to practising living in the present moment, your tomorrows will be as empty as they are today; you simply won't be able to enjoy them. Your habit needs to be worked with. You must condition yourself and your thinking right now as if you were practising any other worthwhile skill. Practise as if the quality of your life depended on it — it does.

The Good News

The good news is that present-moment living can be learned, and it's never too late to start. Remember, when you were a child you were present-moment orientated, so at some internal level you are already familiar with what it feels like. You can start right now, today.

Remind yourself over and over again of how truly wonderful life is when you aren't reviewing past mistakes or worrying about future concerns. Remember that you are in control over what you choose to think about once you understand that you are the thinker of your thoughts. If negative or worrisome thoughts enter your mind, forget about them. If something needs to be dealt with, you will deal with it. I've never met a person who learned to live in the present moment who now feels that her life is falling apart and she is becoming irresponsible. Just the opposite happens. As you stop worrying and start living you will be amazed at how smoothly your life will run. Problems will always be dealt with. No longer will life seem like an emergency. Instead, life will seem like a wonderful dream. Bring your attention back to the only place where you can truly do something about your life anyway — right where you are. Your life is a marvellous gift and you are uniquely wonderful. Don't waste a precious moment producing thoughts of a painful past or an imagined future. When these types of thoughts come up, understand that they are just thoughts and that you don't need to fear them. By all means, learn from your past and then let it go; know that the future will be fine if you approach it one moment at a time. Don't jump the gun, it will be here soon enough.

12

Life is Like a Pendulum

An excellent way to understand where unhappiness exists in your mind and, more important, how to overcome it, is to study the following chart.

Healthy Functioning	Analytical Mind
Living moment to moment	Living in the past or future
Focus is on enjoyment	Focus is on how life could be improved
Mind is clear and free	Mind is full of worry and concern
Seeing the innocence	Seeing the evil
Focusing on the beauty of life	Focusing on the ugliness
Happy with what is	Obsessed with what could be better
Experiencing life	Analysing life
Letting go	Hanging on
Flowing thinking	Computer thinking
Focusing on what you can do	Focusing on what you can't do
Learning from mistakes and going on	Dwelling on mistakes and repeating them
Open and accepting	Closed and prejudiced
Positive attitude	Negative attitude

The left side of this chart is your healthy functioning. Remember your healthy functioning is inherent, you were born with it. Your healthy functioning is your mind when it isn't actively analysing or thinking about what's wrong or finding fault with your life. Healthy functioning feels good and it promotes happiness, self-esteem, and well-being. The moments in your life during which you feel satisfied, when life feels 'just right', you have tapped into this simple, effortless, natural state of mind. It's not mysterious or made up, it's your birthright. Your healthy functioning, although not always recognized, is always present. It lies underneath the veil of negative and insecure thoughts that dominate your mind. The only obstacle to your healthy functioning are the thoughts in your head that you take seriously. *Right now, see if you can gently clear your mind. Relax. Don't think about anything in particular. As thoughts enter your mind, let them go. See them as thoughts and just let them go. How do you feel right now?*

The right side of the chart is your analytical mind. Although your analytical mind is very important, there is nothing natural about it. Every characteristic within this part of your mind is, by definition, learned, or 'thought centred'. You don't naturally live in your past or your future; you learn to do so. You aren't predisposed to focusing on problems; you have developed this habit. You didn't have prejudices at birth; they were learned over time. You weren't born with a negative, pessimistic, and sceptical attitude; you learned it.

The Quiet Mountains and the Barking Dog
Perhaps the best way to understand the difference between your healthy functioning and your analytical mind is to draw an analogy. Imagine yourself in the mountains sitting by a campfire. You are all by yourself

and it's perfectly quiet. You came to the mountains to get some peace and quiet, and you have found it and so much more. You feel like a new person, as though you have regained your perspective on life.

All of a sudden, however, you begin to notice a barking dog way off in the distance. The bark gets louder and louder as you focus your attention on it, and it begins to grate on your nerves. You try to ignore it, but you can't. It goes on and on and on, and gets even louder. 'Why won't he stop?' you think to yourself. 'Why doesn't his owner shut him up?' The distant barking has disturbed your peace and quiet. You begin to feel as though your trip was a waste of time. You forget that you were experiencing the peace and quiet.

Your healthy functioning can be looked at as the peace and quiet you were experiencing before you noticed the dog. The peace and quiet was nothing fancy, it was just quiet and nice. You felt inspired and rejuvenated. You had perspective and you felt a sense of wholeness. If you needed to think, you did so clearly and with wisdom. Your life seemed simple. You saw beauty. You saw answers, not problems.

Your analytical mind can be looked at as the noise of the dog barking in the distance. The more you focused on that, the more it seemed like thunder pounding in your head and the more the noise seemed to dominate your consciousness and take your attention away from your peace and quiet. It seemed as if the dog was right next to you. The noise seemed to be calling out to you, 'Don't enjoy the quiet, listen to me.' Your analytical mind is like a barking dog pleading for your attention. It wants you to listen to it, it wants to be the centre of attention, it doesn't want you to focus on anything else but itself.

Your healthy functioning and your analytical mind are both present at the same time. In our analogy, the quiet of the mountains was still there, it never left the scene. It did, however, become obscured or covered up by the distant noise. Interestingly, the noise of the barking dog (your analytical mind) was there even before you heard it. Like a pendulum, back and forth you swing from the quiet to the barking. The quiet is always there — it brings you peace. The barking is always there — it can drive you crazy. Both are present, but it's your attention, your ability to think, that determines which mode you will experience at any given moment. Do you listen to the noise, or do you listen to the quiet? It's up to you.

Study Children

The next time you get a chance, take a look at a park full of young children — and remember we were all children at one time. Children naturally get along with one another. They do have occasional disputes and arguments, but they usually end up finding ways to have fun together. They don't dwell on mistakes, and yet they have a tremendous ability to learn. They roll with the punches, and treat everyone equally. They see the beauty in life, and virtually everything is a potential source of joy and humour. Children don't care if you are black or white or disabled. Children don't base their happiness on the size of their bank accounts or the size of their parents' bank accounts. They are open to new ideas. If you tell a child that he can't do something, he looks for something else he can do. These are natural qualities that everyone brings to life. They are qualities that can be regained by simply recognizing that the obstacle to them is your own thinking.

Does this mean that children are always happy? Absolutely not! Children have enormous tempers, they can be very selfish and self-centred and they can sulk over almost anything. Children are not always happy because they are human beings. They, like everyone else, react to their own thinking. The difference, however, between children and most adults is that when children get upset they simply get upset and then go on with their lives. They don't label themselves as depressed or angry people. Although their thinking made them upset to begin with, they don't compound the problem by using their thinking to hold their negative feelings in place. They intuitively know that whatever it was that they were upset about is now only a thought. The specifics of the upset aren't important to a child and that is their protection. Whether it was an argument with a sibling or a parent, or something they attempted to do that failed, isn't relevant to a child. What is important is that they don't hold on to the memory as if it were happening right now.

While none of us is always happy, it is nevertheless the case that all of us were born with a natural bent toward the happy side of this pendulum. We were born with a natural curiosity, a desire to grow and learn. We were born with an open and accepting attitude, an innocent and healthy sense of humour. We were born seeing the beauty in our surroundings. If you remove your veil of negative thinking by recognizing that thoughts are just thoughts, and by dismissing your negative thoughts, you will redevelop this childlike attitude and you will feel good again.

As each of us grew older we developed our analytical mind, our own unique thought systems (see Chapter 7). Very simply, through the powers of our own observation, thought, and intellect, we tried to make sense of our world. We put the components of our lives into categories, we labelled people, places, and things, and we developed an attitude towards life.

As I explained in chapter 7, there is nothing wrong with your thought system. You must have one and your interpretation of life seems every bit as real to you as mind does to me. As it developed, you saw what you saw and you tried to make sense out of it. As I pointed out earlier, the problem isn't that you have a thought system, the problem is that it's very difficult to question it. Therefore, you tend to believe whatever you think. True freedom comes when you begin to distrust, just a little, your thought-created version of life. As you do, you will naturally tune into a deeper, wiser part of yourself — your healthy functioning.

It is important to realize that everyone has both healthy functioning and a learned state of mind. The pendulum I'm referring to is the swinging between your healthy functioning and your analytical mind during the course of a day. There is nothing any of us can do to make either of them go away because both of them are an integral part of being human. We can, however, learn to discredit the validity of parts of our thought system when it comes to matters of happiness and well-being. We can also learn to direct our attention towards our healthy functioning — swing the pendulum if you will — when what we are experiencing isn't what we would like. Too few of us realize that this other part of us, this healthy functioning, is every bit as real and present as our thought system and is crucial to our happiness and peace of mind.

While you are experiencing your healthy functioning, however, you are still producing thoughts. If a thought enters your mind and you follow that thought, you are at risk of swinging the pendulum in the other direction. The goal is to become conscious about which trains of thought to follow. You want to be able to decide for yourself if, and when, you swing the pendulum back to your thought system.

How Do You Swing the Pendulum?

Many depressed people believe they are always depressed. My experience, however, has shown me that this is not true. Even severely depressed people have pendulum swings, moments in the day when they are experiencing healthy functioning. Even 30 seconds of inner peace is a swing in the pendulum. Many happy people who used to be depressed have told me, 'Looking back, I can see that I *did* experience moments of healthy functioning, I simply never recognized it.' The moments are there. When you fail to recognize them, however, a single insecure thought can encourage your mind to start spinning once again. Because this dynamic happens so quickly, and so automatically, you may incorrectly conclude that you are always depressed.

In many respects it's far more important to recognize when you are in a state of healthy functioning than to recognize when you are stuck in your analytical mind. As you recognize healthy functioning for what it is you encourage more of it in your life. Recognizing healthy functioning is a preventive measure. It helps you become familiar with what it feels like to feel good. There is clearly a domino effect that takes place — one minute of positive feeling leads to another and then another and so on.

The same domino effect can apply to negative feelings, which is precisely why you *never* want to dwell on negative feelings. As you think about how bad you feel, and as you focus attention on that feeling, you are in effect asking for more of the same. If you want to feel good you must learn to detect and then follow your good feelings.

When you do find yourself trapped in your analytical mind, stuck on the right-hand side of the chart, the best you can do is drop your thoughts, clear your mind, and relax. Your problem is clear: you are caught up in your thinking. You don't need to know anything else. Whether you are caught up in thoughts about a relationship, money, sex, or your past isn't relevant. What is relevant is the fact that you are caught up. Analysing what you think is wrong will only make matters worse. Whatever thoughts you are thinking will grow in your mind as you study them. And as your thoughts grow, you will feel worse and worse. You will unknowingly be cementing yourself onto the analytical side of the pendulum.

Your healthy functioning is the most important part of your life. If you align yourself with your healthy functioning, your personality will right itself. Yet, no amount of work that you put into your personality will affect your healthy functioning. It's worth the effort to become aware of your healthy functioning. It's all you need to live a fully functional, happy life.

While we have no control over the fact that we have both healthy functioning and an analytical mind, we do have control over where we choose to put our greatest amount of attention. Certainly there are many instances when using your intellect is preferable to using your healthy functioning: learning some new skill, balancing your cheque-book, fixing the electricity, trying to remember a phone number or where you left your car. In these instances, putting your attention on your thinking mind is necessary and desirable. Surprisingly, however, a vast part of your life would be far better lived and experienced without your 'computer' turned on. You can't enjoy life if you are analysing it; you can't smell the roses if you are running past them; you can't enjoy new people if you prejudge them; you can't have fun doing simple things if you are thinking about how stupid they are; you can't be relaxed if you are worried about what might happen; you can't enjoy your work if you are comparing yourself to others; and you can't even enjoy your weekends or holidays if you are walking around generating concerns all day long.

The only thing that stands between you and a completely different experience of life — a life without depression — is your ability to realize that each moment, especially those moments when depression is looming, is a potential swing of the pendulum, a choice point (see Chapter 8). You can focus your attention on your bad feelings and keep the pendulum on the negative side of your psychological scale, keeping it alive, nursing it, almost as though you want it to stay with you. Or you can ignore (even if it doesn't initially seem possible) the negative feelings that you are having, realizing they are thought-created, and swing the pendulum back towards your healthy functioning, thereby tapping into the part of yourself that doesn't experience depression, that feels peace and love, and is filled with wisdom.

The only thing that can defeat you is a lack of persistence on your part. The first few times you challenge your tendency to give in to your depressed feelings you may not notice an immediate or particularly strong shift in how you feel because you may not be letting go enough. But stick with it — it gets much easier. As you practise ignoring what you don't want, and turn instead towards what you do want, you will soon begin to feel a shift.

As you get the hang of it, and practise controlling the focus of your attention, you will see that life really is like a pendulum, and it really is about choice. You go through shifts in consciousness, shifts in how you feel, throughout each day. The shifts are completely harmless and, in fact, are quite natural. The harm, or pain, comes from your studying, thinking about, and focusing on the thought-created feelings that you don't want anything to do with. As you see the dynamic, and as you practise working with the natural flow of the pendulum, you will become less and less frightened by your own feelings, thereby dispensing with the ones you no longer want, while nurturing the ones you do want. Life will become interesting and rich again because you will be turning towards something greater than that to which you are accustomed, to a more powerful and genuine part of yourself that knows the joy of happiness.

Your Feelings are Your Guide

Your feelings let you know which side of your mind you are on at any given moment, thus telling you whether you need to make a mental adjustment. If you feel peaceful, in control, competent, balanced, happy, contented, and satisfied, you know that emotionally you are on the healthier side. No adjustment needs to be made. Keep right on living. You will make great decisions, you will look after your own best interests, you will be kind, considerate, and easy-going. When decisions need to be made, you will be level-headed, even if the decisions are difficult. If, however, you find yourself feeling depressed, bothered, agitated, frustrated, rushed, hurried, defensive, jealous, angry, frightened, or in some other way immobilized, your feelings let you know that you have shifted over to the more familiar side of your emotional scale.

Let me make something very clear. There's absolutely nothing wrong with being on that familiar side of the emotional scale. I'm not suggesting that it's never appropriate or even important to have these various feelings. It is critical, however, that you realize these emotions are thought-created and that they are learned. If you hadn't learned to feel defensive, for example, you wouldn't feel defensive. There is nothing inherent in you that makes you feel this way. The same is true with pessimism. Regardless of how it happened, you learned to be pessimistic.

You don't need to judge yourself on how often or how long you spend in your analytical mind. No one is keeping score. In fact, the less you keep score, the easier it will be to swing yourself in the direction of your choice. Knowing where you are emotionally is important. If you use your feelings to your advantage, and you recognize when you are off track, you will at least have the option of looking for something else. If, on the other hand, you get into your feelings simply because they are there, you will have no options available to you. You will have to struggle with your thinking each time you experience a negative emotion.

When you allow your negative feelings to alert you that you are emotionally off track, you can begin to direct your attention away from your analytical mind where the problem started, and instead bring your attention towards your healthy functioning where the solution exists, where you gain some perspective and look for an answer.

Your feelings, even your negative ones, can help guide you through your life. By paying attention to them, yet never dwelling on the negative ones, you can use them to help swing your emotional pendulum in your favour. As you turn your attention away from your thinking mind when you are in emotional trouble, your life will settle down and look beautiful once again. Your lows won't seem so bad and they certainly won't last as long. In fact, you can become quite comfortable when you are down — when you know that going back up is just a matter of time.

13

Mental Health and the Dynamics of Unhappiness

As we have seen, the state of mental health is characterized by feelings of well-being that are innate within each of us. We have called this positive state of mind 'healthy functioning'. These deep human feelings do not depend on any external circumstance, on life being any certain way. Thus, mental health is never completely lost, and doesn't have to fluctuate depending on what is happening in a person's life. In a state of mental health, we intuitively understand the nature of thought and how it workss to create our personal reality — our happiness and our unhappiness. When this happens, we are no longer victims of the content of our own thinking. Instead, we rise above the content of our thoughts to a place where we are free from its effects.

Mental problems and unhappiness are the result of an individual becoming overly absorbed by the content of his own negative thinking, while at the same time being unaware that he is thinking. Each time this occurs, the individual involved will be at the mercy of the specific content of his own thinking. If his thinking is negative, so too will be the feelings he experiences. However, because he is unaware that *he* is the producer of those feelings via his own thinking, he will place the blame for those feelings on external sources rather than on the negative thinking itself, which originates within himself. The usual result is that the individual tries to understand *why* he feels so bad by thinking about what would make him feel better, or how he could alter his environment to improve his life. Unfortunately, when a person is already feeling bad, this will always initiate a vicious cycle wherein the individual sustains his negative reality by wondering how or when it could be different.

You are probably beginning to see the hopelessness of trying to think your way out of negative feelings. You can't do it. Mental health, or positive feelings, are always present but become obscured by negative thinking. The more you think about the problem or how you feel, the more lost you will become within your own thoughts. The thoughts themselves are the problem, not the solution.

The way out of this negative loop is to stop generating negative thoughts. Many people respond to this suggestion by saying 'Easier said than done,' but in fact this is not as difficult as it seems, as soon as you realize that you are the one producing the negative thoughts to begin with. The thoughts you are having originate within yourself yourself are not the result of some external condition.

Unhappiness is a result of negative thinking that results in negative feelings and, often, negative behaviour. An important point to understand is this: *the very moment a person drops his negative thought process, that person experiences an immediate shift in the way he feels – for the better.* For example, suppose you have a heated argument with a co-worker that results in you leaving the conversation in a huff. You storm out of the room and as you drive home steaming mad you review the argument in your mind over and over again. As you think about the conflict, you feel the negative effects of your thinking — you get angrier and more frustrated. As you walk into your house, however, the phone is ringing and you rush over to answer it. A dear friend is on the line who you haven't spoken to in over a year. You are distracted, your attention is shifted away from the problem, and for all practical purposes, it disappears. While you are on the phone, your problem is forgotten.

When anything is forgotten or dismissed, it means that it does not exist in your mind. And if something doesn't exist in your mind, it doesn't exist in your reality and you are not affected by it. The only way to bring that reality back to yourself is to think about it again.

Labelling yourself as unhappy is a dangerous thing to do. Your personal reality consists of that which you think about. The act of labelling your feelings keeps the thoughts of how bad you feel alive in your mind. Again, *thinking is the source of the problem.*

In terms of learning to eliminate unhappiness, a critical distinction needs to be made between a principle and details. A principle is what is applicable regardless of the specifics of any situation. The details, of course, are the variables that differ from one situation to the next. In our example above, you would have been freed of your negative feelings prior to receiving your phone call from your friend the moment you realized that you were creating your own angry feelings by keeping the argument alive in your thinking. This is true regardless of what the argument happened to be about, how long it lasted, how bad it was, the looks on your co-worker's face, and so on. This is key to understanding the principle of how thought works.

If, however, you had gone to a traditional psycho-therapist to deal with this issue, you would undoubtedly have been instructed to focus on and deal with the specific details involved such as how you felt during the argument, after the argument, and so forth.

Understanding the principle of thought allows you to set aside the confusing details that go along with any problem so that you can see how to stop generating your mental anguish in the first place. The details of your problems don't matter in terms of learning how to be less affected by them. They apply only to specific issues. The content of your thoughts becomes a problem only when you forget that they are just thoughts.

The dynamics of unhappiness are best understood as a principle which is always the same. The only obstacles standing in the way of mental health are negative and insecure thoughts that we become absorbed into. Without realizing that we are the producers of those thoughts, we are victims of our own thinking. When we understand, however, that we are putting on our own show, we become empowered to improve the quality of our lives. Whatever the specific thoughts that make us unhappy, they are still only thoughts. And as thoughts, they have no power to hurt us.

Genuine Sadness
You may be thinking, if the cause of our negative feelings and unhappiness is always our own thinking, is there any legitimacy in feeling sadness? The answer is an absolute *yes*. It's important, however, to draw a distinction between genuine sadness and becoming immobilized by your own thinking to the point of becoming unhappy for an extended period of time.

Genuine sadness is a natural part of life. There is nothing unhealthy about it. Sadness results whenever you feel a sense of loss or disappointment. Suppose, for example, your child is hurt in an accident. It's crazy to assume you wouldn't feel any sadness about this event. Of course you would. The sadness you did feel would include feelings of concern, compassion, and, perhaps, gratitude. In this way, sadness is a very positive feeling. It reminds you of what you have, or in some cases what you had. Sadness isn't something to run or hide from, it's real and important. It adds tremendous depth to your life.

As I will explain in chapter 14, the feeling of sadness comes and goes. It's not permanent, and it does not necessarily have to lead to a feeling of despair or hopelessness. In order for sadness to turn into unhappiness, depression, or hopelessness, you would have to hold on to the thoughts about the event you were experiencing. So, as in the above example, instead of feeling sadness about your child's accident and then moving on, you might continue or even magnify your thoughts about the event until they began to overwhelm you. Thoughts like 'Oh my God, what am I going to do if she doesn't get better?' begin to fill your head. As you pay further attention to these additional thoughts about the event, your genuine sadness transforms itself into a negative state of mind.

It boils down to this: *genuine sadness can lead to a feeling of love, whereas getting caught in the dynamic of unhappiness usually leads to self-pity and hopelessness.* If you can see that it's not only possible, but in fact desirable to feel sadness without becoming immobilized by it, you will be on your way to experiencing all negative events in an entirely new way. It just takes a little practice at dismissing the extra thoughts that keep the sadness alive.

When a painful event takes place, such as the breakup of a relationship, it's as though you are at a fork in the road. One direction, the 'high road', leads to growth and gratitude; the other, the 'low road', leads straight to the emotional dump. The direction you take depends entirely on your level of understanding.

The high road allows you to feel the sense of loss, yet when thoughts like 'Why me?' enter your mind, you dismiss them. In this way, you'll still feel the sadness, but the severity and duration of your sadness will be limited, and your sadness won't turn into an ongoing negative state of mind. Dismissing these thoughts isn't the same as denial. You are dismissing your negative thoughts for one reason alone — to reconnect with your healthy functioning. When you do, your wisdom will tell you what to do next.

The low road involves feeling your sadness but also paying attention to the painful thoughts that keep entering your mind. Without consciously deciding to dismiss your painful thoughts, the thoughts will feed upon one another. 'Why me?' will be followed by any number of other negative, painful thoughts that will soon act like a snowball rolling down a mountain. One thought will lead to another and then another. Pretty soon, your entire mind is filled with sadness and self-pity.

The only way to avoid this dynamic is to be acutely aware that this is what will happen *unless* you consciously decide to dismiss your sad thoughts as they enter your mind. Anyone can handle the thought 'Why me?' The hard part is when one sad thought turns into ten sad thoughts.

Many people honestly believe that it's natural to feel depressed, overwhelmed, frustrated, or immobilized when certain events take place, such as the loss of a loved one, a terminal disease, a breakup, or a divorce. This is not necessarily the case. What *is* true is that it's natural to feel sadness. But, as we have seen, sadness doesn't necessarily have to turn into all-out negativity.

Understanding thought and the dynamics of unhappiness allows us to feel the natural human feelings that we all share without allowing these feelings to get the better of us. This understanding does not involve ignoring or repressing natural emotions, but rather learning that feelings and thoughts need not overwhelm us. Instead, you can learn to use your feelings as a navigational tool to guide you through difficult times and point you towards contentment.

14

Grief and Loss

We have to come to an important distinction that lies at the heart of learning to feel better. This distinction has to do with the difference between having painful thoughts and turning those painful thoughts into a negative state of mind. The purpose of this chapter is to show you that you can have one without the other.

Whenever something painful occurs in your life, such as a loss of some kind, you are quite naturally going to have thoughts about that event. Many of these thoughts are going to be painful thoughts, thoughts of regret, confusion, or loss. The specific content of these painful thoughts will, of course, vary from person to person.

Thoughts, in and of themselves, painful or not, have no reality to them. They are just thoughts. If your painful thoughts come and go, they will be like all your other thoughts. They will enter your mind and then float from your consciousness. For example, after losing someone you love you might have the thought, 'I'll never see her again. I'm going to miss her.' With these thoughts you will feel a corresponding emotional feeling, in this case, sadness, which is natural.

The nature of thoughts is that they do come and go. In this example, the thought 'I'll never see her again. I'm going to miss her,' will drift from your consciousness — and a minute later you will be having a different set of thoughts. The new thoughts might be related to your sense of loss, or they might be unrelated. You can see that as thoughts cross your mind and drift away naturally, they are harmless. Your knowledge of the passing nature of thoughts is the factor that allows them to pass more quickly and drift from your consciousness. In other words, because you know that your painful thoughts are only temporary, they have less negative impact on your state of mind and don't stay with you as long. Because you know they are temporary, you are able to pay less attention to them.

If, instead of letting these thoughts drift through your mind, you hold onto them, make them real and give them significance by paying them undue attention, they will stay present in your mind until they become a depression.

As a thought stays with you it begins to take its effect on the way you feel. Even a thought about a minor issue such as a person driving too slowly in front of you can send you crazy if it doesn't leave your mind quickly enough. We have the ability, if we so choose, to make any thoughts as permanent as we wish. This is precisely why so many people live in an almost constant state of frustration and irritation — often over trivial things. They think about something and hang on to the thought as if doing so was somehow going to help.

People who find themselves in this predicament often come to the conclusion that the object of their thinking (i.e. the slow driver in front of you) is the cause of their negative feeling. This isn't true. The slow driver is long gone and out of the picture — other than in your own mind. The *actual cause* of the negative feeling you are experiencing is the *excess thought* about the driver. If you had dismissed the thoughts that entered your mind instead of focused on them, you may have felt some slight irritation, but the event wouldn't have turned into a negative feeling state. The same cause for unhappiness is true whether your issue is a painful past, an uncertain future, a feeling of hopelessness, an ungrateful spouse, too much responsibility, or not enough money. *It's always the thoughts you have about events, not the events themselves that create the feelings you experience.* You can have thoughts about *any* issue, no matter how painful it may be, and be shielded from feeling bad. Your thoughts cannot hurt you as long as you remember that you are the thinker of your own thoughts and that your thoughts are creating the feelings you are experiencing. As long as you let these thoughts come and go, their effect on you will be minimal.

A 'feeling state' is a state of mind that comes about by keeping thoughts at the front of your mind. Any time you hold on to or dwell on a thought, be it positive or negative, you shift from a state of passing thoughts, which have no potential to harm you, to a state of mind or 'feeling state' which does have the potential to harm you.

If we let them simmer in our minds, our thoughts will create the feelings we experience. A passing thought such as 'My husband might be having an affair' has no power to hurt you. If, however, that identical thought is repeated, if it leads to other similar, related thoughts and analysis of all the negative possibilities, discussion with a therapist about your fears, and so forth, this same innocent and harmless thought can turn into a feeling state of insecurity, jealousy, or fear. The thought itself was harmless — and you could very well have let it pass away like all your other thoughts. It's what you do with a thought, and how you relate to a thought, not the thought itself, that determines how you are going to feel and react.

It's more difficult to get *out* of a negative feeling state than it is to prevent yourself from getting into one.

Once you understand the dynamics of thought, preventing negative feeling states can be very simple. In the same way that you would turn down a glass of water that was offered to you if your thirst was already quenched, you can learn to let thoughts drift from your mind if your mind has had enough. Once you know the end result of dwelling on your thoughts — a feeling state — overthinking loses its appeal.

Even though it can be difficult to pull yourself out of a negative feeling state, it is possible, once you see where the negativity stems from — in your own thoughts. When you are already in a negative state of mind, negativity is all you see. The negativity itself, however, always stems from the same place. It stems from holding onto whatever negative thoughts you were having. Simple thoughts like 'I'll never be any good at that' can be dismissed and let go of, or they can be focused on, studied, analysed, or dwelt upon. If you let go of this thought, let it pass through your mind like other thoughts, the effect on your emotional well-being will be insignificant. If, however, you make something of the thought, study it, and give it significance, you will have opened the door for unnecessary and almost certain pain. We all do this to ourselves, to various extents, every day. With proper understanding, however, we can reduce, to a large degree, this self-inflicted pain and suffering.

The most difficult part of this understanding to grasp, and something that is absolutely critical to understand, is that when you are feeling low, you will rarely realize what you have done to yourself. You probably won't realize that you have held on to a negative thought, or series of negative thoughts, to the point of turning those thoughts into a negative feeling state. You probably won't realize that you have turned a passing thought into an 'institution' in your mind. Instead, you will be tempted to believe, even argue the point, 'I wasn't thinking negatively, I just feel bad. I have real problems.' In order to implement this understanding fully, you *must* see where *all* negative feeling states come from — thought. It's really an all-or-nothing understanding. You must see that it's impossible to feel jealous without first having jealous thoughts, it's impossible to feel angry without first having angry thoughts, it's impossible to feel worried without first having worried thoughts, and it's impossible to feel depressed without first having depressing thoughts. I know this sounds obvious, but in a way it's not. Because thoughts and feelings are so closely linked, it's very difficult to see what's happening to yourself — while it's happening. The time it takes to link negative thoughts together to create a negative feeling state is about the same as the amount of time it takes to flick on a light switch and see the light — it's instant. It's important to understand that there are no exceptions to this principle, even when it seems as though there are. It's always going to seem as though a negative feeling state exists on its own — as if it just happened to you out of the blue. It didn't! It stemmed from thoughts that were kept in your mind too long. The good news is that because feeling states stem from your own thoughts, you can learn to have control over the feeling state you are in by learning to dismiss negative thoughts as they enter your mind.

The mind doesn't deal very well in abstractions. When you aren't feeling emotionally well, your mind, in an attempt to explain its predicament, attaches itself to something tangible. So rather than just allowing yourself simply to feel bad knowing that your negative feelings came from your own thoughts, your mind searches for a more sophisticated explanation. 'I feel bad *because* my life is no good,' or 'I feel bad *because* I am sick,' become the so-called reasons for our misery. The mind only does this out of habit. The reasons we come up with seem to us, and to everyone else, to make complete sense, so we continue believing in them. We think about the reasons frequently, we talk to others about the reasons, and so forth. We do this without realizing that although we are searching for a solution to our problems, what we are really doing is making ourselves feel worse by finding explanations for our unhappiness. Once you know that the reasons you come up with *aren't* the cause of your misery — but that your mind's reaction to those reasons is — you can't help but feel better.

The mind is very persistent in its efforts to explain why we feel bad. As one explanation proves meaningless in terms of making you feel better, the mind will search for another explanation. If the thought 'The reason I'm unhappy is that I have the wrong mate' doesn't help, the mind tries again: 'The reason I'm unhappy is that I had a terrible childhood.' The mind will search and search for the right answer, when in fact the right answer is always the same. It's your thoughts about events — not the events themselves — that make them seem painful. If your painful thoughts can come and go, all events can be looked at with the same perspective and understanding. The other option is to continue to dwell on the reasons you feel bad. Unfortunately, this option becomes a way of life for many.

No one likes pain and suffering and no one wants to feel bad. The difference between a person who can experience painful events in their life in a 'healthy' way — meaning they get through painful events gracefully — and those people who become immobilized by similar events has to do with their relationship to their own thoughts. The question is, can you have thoughts, even negative ones, and let them pass? Or do you hold on to your thoughts, interfering with the natural flow and rhythm of your thoughts, to the point of letting your thoughts hurt your emotional life? The other question to ask yourself is, can you recognize that thoughts are just thoughts, images you create in your mind? Or do you believe that if thoughts enter your mind you must entertain and give significance to them, as if they had a life of their own? Your answer to these questions will determine your ability to learn to pull yourself out of a negative feeling state. If you can allow yourself to have whatever thoughts you have, while at the same time maintaining the understanding that your thoughts are not reality and cannot affect you in a negative way, you will be able to let them pass.

When you have a healthy relationship to your own thinking, you can have an unlimited number of negative thoughts pass through your mind. No matter how strong, painful, or compelling your thoughts may be, you are still able to see them as just thoughts. As long as you let your thoughts come and go, and as long as you don't make more out of them than they really are, you will always feel OK and have a sense of perspective. Even your most difficult times won't be as hard as they would otherwise be, and you will be able to pull yourself out of negative feeling states.

Sarah had been despondent for many months after the death of her father. In therapy she was told that grief was natural and necessary and that she should continue to 'get in touch with her feelings'. And while this advice is in part true, her therapist never told Sarah that the degree of her grief was determined solely by the thoughts she was having about her deceased father. While she was thinking about the loss of her father she would feel her grief, but while she was going about her day, thinking about other things, the grief wouldn't be present. In other words, the grief itself wasn't a permanent institution in her life, it was a fluctuating and constantly changing phenomenon. Sarah did learn to get in touch with her feelings, but unfortunately that was all she learned. She was *so* in touch with her painful feelings that she couldn't feel anything else. When she asked her therapist to help her, the suggestion was given, 'You haven't gone deep enough into your pain.'

When Sarah contacted me, she wanted to know whether the principles I teach applied to 'serious, real-life problems'. Working with Sarah was very simple. She learned the essence of what we have been covering in this chapter: sometimes grief can be overwhelming, other times it will be minor, and often it won't be there at all. The idea that sometimes her grief wasn't there at all turned out to be very significant for Sarah. She had been taught in therapy that if she wasn't feeling bad, she wasn't being true to her real feelings! Her response to this suggestion was to feel guilty and to focus on her painful thoughts *all the time* so that she would be 'properly grieving'. Her therapist's advice was utter nonsense! The truth is, Sarah *was* being true to her feelings. What she didn't understand, and what she needed to know, was that her negative feelings were only present while she was thinking about her father. She didn't realize that it was healthy and natural not to feel bad all the time. Grieving, Sarah learned, is a process whereby one feels bad some of the time, but not all of the time! It's silly to believe that only your negative feelings are your 'real' feelings.

This insight came as a tremendous relief for Sarah, who had been led to believe that grieving was something that existed on its own, something permanent that would disappear only through the passage of time. Grief quickly became a beautiful experience for Sarah. She now understood that the feelings she was having were temporary and ever-changing, and learned not to be frightened and depressed by them. She developed a sense of gratitude about her father that had been suppressed by her powerful feelings of grief.

It's not that Sarah's negative feelings weren't real or justified — they most certainly were. But Sarah had been so overwhelmed by her own thoughts that she had lost sight of the beautiful feelings she had for her father. Warm, grateful feelings were the way Sarah wanted to remember him. Fortunately, she is now able to do just that.

The Content of your Thoughts isn't Relevant

Everyone has their own unique and important story to tell. Almost everyone feels that the specific details of their life, certain significant events and occurrences, explain why they feel unhappy. They point to their past, their present circumstances, their issues, their problems, or their uncertain future as the cause of their suffering. The general feeling is that if you can explore and resolve these issues, your happiness will magically appear. Although many people find this difficult to accept, it's nevertheless true — and it's critical if you want to learn to have control over how you feel — that *the specific content of your negative thoughts isn't relevant.* Whether your negative thoughts have to do with being mistreated, losing your job, financial strain, relationship difficulty, grief and loss, or simply the general thoughts you have about how hard life is, the *underlying* issue has to do with what you did with those thoughts and how you relate to those thoughts, not the thoughts themselves. This understanding is critical because you will always have an unlimited supply of painful examples that can be drummed up and seen as the exception to this rule. You can always convince yourself of things like, 'It's true that thoughts are just thoughts — but these thoughts are more important than all the others. After all, I have real problems.' You will always be able to point to the one, serious or painful event that you can't forget, or that doesn't apply.

One person might have lost her husband in a car crash and another might have been abused as a child. Both are unquestionably painful and difficult situations to have had to have gone through. No one would deny that both are circumstances that everyone would hope to avoid, and we can certainly have compassion for those who go through them. However, if the person who lost her husband is aware of her healthy functioning and is able to let her thoughts about the event pass through her mind, and the person who was abused as a child holds on to her thoughts, as if her negative experiences were happening all over again, the person who lost her husband will fare better than the person who was abused, in terms of feeling good and enjoying her life. Like Sarah, the person who lost her husband in a car crash is going to have plenty of painful thoughts to contend with. The question is going to be how she relates to her thoughts. Does she let them come and go, or does she give those thoughts too much attention and keep them in the front of her mind?

Keep in mind as you take in this material that the woman who lost her husband is *not* denying or pretending that the event itself wasn't terribly painful, nor is she pretending that the memory of the event isn't painful. She is simply acknowledging her thoughts and feelings, knowing that she has the potential to let her thoughts come and go. She is aware that when she is engaged in her healthy functioning, she will feel OK, and her memory of her husband will be an inspiring instead of regretful experience. If she didn't know about healthy functioning, and about her ability to let go of her thoughts, and instead held on to them, she almost certainly would turn her passing thoughts into a negative feeling state, if not a state of downright depression. The harder she held on, the more painful her recovery would be.

Even a support group or therapist whose intentions are purely good can potentially harm a 'victim' by encouraging her to think about and talk about her thoughts, as if those thoughts had a life of their own. Remember, 'thought' is your ability to create images in your own mind. The images themselves are not real. If you know they are just images — and your therapist or support group shares this understanding — then discussing or thinking about the painful events in your life (which are now only images) can be liberating, inspiring, even beautiful. But thinking about and discussing painful events for the sake of getting into your pain is downright dangerous. It can turn an already unhappy event such as the loss of a loved one into a nightmare.

Imagine, for a moment, a five-year-old child who tells you about the 'bad man' who lives behind his books on his bookshelf. Would you have him explain in great detail, over and over again, what the bad man looks like, what kinds of things he does, and why he's so scary? Would you ask the child these questions every week, for years and years? Of course not. The reason you wouldn't is because you would be making the child's imagination seem real to him. *You would be encouraging him to be frightened by his own thoughts!* It would be far more useful to the child if you were to help him see that there is no need to fear his own thoughts.

The only difference between a child's imagination and real events is that the real events happened — once. Right now, however, in real life, in this moment, imagined events along with events that really did happen or that might happen are just thoughts in the mind.

Many years ago, one of the best friends I've ever had, along with his lovely female companion, were tragically killed by a drunk driver on their way to my wedding party. This was a truly tragic event, one that I will never forget. My love for this friend will forever be in my heart as will my compassion for his wonderful family. There are very few days that go by that I don't have passing thoughts about our tremendous friendship, or thoughts of loss and sadness.

Even years later, when these thoughts pass through my mind, I have moments of sadness or loss. As the thoughts drift through my mind, however, I know they are just passing thoughts. I never pretend that the thoughts aren't with me, nor do I even want them to go away. I just allow them to drift away, the same way that other thoughts drift away. I never forget that they are just thoughts. This doesn't diminish the love I feel or the gratitude I have for his place in my life. In fact, just the opposite is true. I can afford emotionally to cherish his memory because my thoughts don't frighten me, nor do they lower my spirits. If I were frightened or overly saddened by my thoughts about my friend, I would have to avoid thinking about him. This would reduce the gratitude I have in my heart — something I would never choose to do.

What if Thoughts Need to be Addressed?
What do you do when a specific thought or series of thoughts really needs to be addressed? You certainly can't nor would you want to dismiss *every* thought that goes through your mind. Often it's appropriate and desirable to think about something.

When you have the understanding that thoughts are just thoughts, that they have no life of their own, and you know that you have the power to let thoughts pass, you are protected, to a very large degree, from the effects of those thoughts. For example, you might have the thought, 'My husband hasn't been very kind to me lately.' The fact that you have this thought doesn't necessarily mean you shouldn't ponder it further. Maybe you should. You are always in the driver's seat when you remember that *you* are the one doing the thinking! As you remember that you are the thinker, and as you remember that it's your thoughts, not your husband, that are making you feel the way you do, you create new options in your life. You can continue to think about your husband — why he hasn't been kind to you, or perhaps that there is something wrong with him — but if you begin to feel a little overwhelmed by your own thinking, you can let the thoughts go and always choose to return to them later.

When you let go of thoughts that are taking you into a negative feeling state, you are not sacrificing your ability to deal with a situation. In the case of our example about the unkind husband, you have already entered the necessary information into your memory. The fact that you have stopped thinking about how unkind he has been will open the door to your wisdom, and you will know what to do about the situation. You may decide to talk to your husband, you may decide to become more observant, or you may decide to do nothing, for now. You'll know, because your wisdom, or common sense, isn't tied exclusively to your intellect; it comes from a different place — a place of quiet in your consciousness.

If you're having financial trouble or some other worry, the best you can do is to acknowledge the problem and the thoughts you are having, and then just *know* that you need an answer. If you trust your wisdom, it will always tell you whether you need to seek another career, improve your existing skills, or find some other solution. Thinking about the problem to excess will only lower your spirits further, making a solution less likely. If you absolutely must think about the problem, do so *knowing* that you are the one doing the thinking. You are the one dictating how you are feeling based entirely on how many thoughts you are letting pass and how many you are holding on to.

The goal of this understanding is *not* to deny your experience, nor is it about trying to get rid of your thoughts. In fact, it's just the opposite; it's about opening to your experience. There is nothing to be frightened of regarding your own thoughts or feelings — there is nothing they can do to hurt you.

This understanding is about learning to accept thoughts for what they are. There is no need to turn them into more than they really are or to take them too seriously. In all likelihood, you will spend some moments, every day for the rest of your life, thinking at least a few negative, fearful, or painful thoughts. When you understand the harmless nature of thoughts, you can come to peace with your own thinking. You can openly accept whatever thoughts happen to be in your mind, and as they pass through your mind in a healthier manner, the feelings you have about those thoughts will begin to change, and a softness and inner peace will come about. Rather than being frightened or overwhelmed by thoughts you are having, you will maintain a sense of perspective.

As long as you can let your thoughts come and go, you will notice that effect of those thoughts on your well-being will be minimal. You will spend more time in your healthy functioning and less time absorbed in your own thoughts. When you must deal with something as difficult as grief and loss, it's critical to remember that even painful thoughts will drift away — and when they do you can return to your healthy psychological functioning and to a state of contentment.

15

Illness and Death

When considering a serious illness or the anticipation of death with a terminal illness, you will notice a striking similarity, in an emotional sense, to the consideration of grief and loss. The difference between these life-events is that grief and loss have to do with something painful that has already happened, whereas dealing with impending death has to do with something painful that is yet to happen. Illness, of course, has to do with something that is happening right now.

The dynamics of thought do not change when you are facing an illness or death, or any other painful event that is yet to happen or is happening now. It is still the thoughts you have about the illness or death that create your emotional disturbance — not the illness or death itself. This is the key to understanding what distinguishes a person who can accept the painful parts of life and move on from a person who becomes immobilized by the same set of facts. Obviously, no one likes to deal with the painful parts of life, but those who understand the dynamics of their own thinking are far more equipped to handle them.

Like all thoughts, you will notice that your thoughts about illness and death will come and go. There will be times when you think about your predicament and times when you think about something else. There will be times when you feel sad, angry, or frustrated, and there will be other times when you feel OK. The important point is this: *if your physical condition was actually causing your emotional pain then you, and everyone else facing a similar trauma, would be in emotional pain all the time.* But this isn't true. The emotional pain you experience will come and go with your thoughts. As you become able to witness the partnership between your thoughts and your pain — as well as the relationship between a lack of thoughts and your lack of pain — you will gradually be able to relax and let go when you are experiencing pain. A client of mine who was about to lose his spouse to death put it this way: 'I used to be a complete victim of whatever thoughts were crossing my mind, like a ship in a violent storm without a wheel. Now I feel like the captain of my own ship. My wheel is my understanding that my thoughts are creating my pain. I now have at least some control over my thoughts. It's not that I never experience pain — I most certainly do — but my perspective is entirely different. I know that I am navigating my own ship. The storm is much calmer.'

If you or someone you love is facing death or confronting the implications of a serious illness, it is certainly going to be difficult. However, the fact that you must go through such an experience is all the more reason to learn to live the rest of your life with a peaceful inner feeling, rather than being consumed by your illness. Understanding the dynamics of thought is the way to go about achieving a sense of inner peace.

Ram Dass, a Western philosopher who is known for his ability to comfort individuals who are dying, told a story about a woman he was working with who was dying of cancer. With only a few weeks left to live, this dear woman was spending virtually all of her available energy thinking about and discussing how awful it was to be dying. Ram Dass said something to her that speaks rather pointedly to the issue of anticipating death: 'Do you think it would be possible to spend less time dying and more time living?' The first moment he said this to her, the woman was offended and angry. 'How could you be so insensitive and cruel?' she said. But a few moments later, after seeing the sincerity in Ram Dass's eyes, she tapped into the spirit of what he was saying. 'You are right,' she said, 'I've been so busy dying that I completely forgot to live.' One week later the woman died. Before she died, however, she told Ram Dass, 'I have lived more this last week than in all my previous days.'

Many people, myself included, have been criticized for suggesting that a person who is suffering or dying could possibly find a sense of inner contentment. The criticism usually comes in the form of a question such as 'How could you possibly understand what it's like to suffer?' This criticism is understandable, especially when it is delivered by someone who is personally suffering. However, it's important to know that people who are suffering don't want to be suffering. They want to learn how to live, even if there is very little time left to do so.

When you are anticipating anything, even something as difficult to accept as death, it is just that — anticipation. To anticipate means to 'look forward', to *think* about what it yet to be. Anticipating death isn't death itself, it's your thoughts about death. In this moment, death is but an image in your mind — a thought.

To illustrate the point, consider a person who isn't facing a serious or terminal illness but who lives in fear of becoming ill. There are millions of people who spend most of their waking day thinking about something that doesn't even exist. Yet to these individuals the fear is often as real as for those who truly do face an illness. Such is the power of thought. Whether you are sick or well, your thinking can help you or it can destroy your life. The critical issue in terms of emotional well-being isn't your physical health, or the circumstances of your life, but the relationship you have to your own thinking, what you make of your circumstances. Do you focus on every fearful thought that enters your mind? Do you spend the precious moments of life anticipating death? Or can you learn that thoughts — even the most painful ones — are just thoughts and that you can dismiss them when you choose to do so?

This is not a prescription for denial. If you are sick or dying you *must* face the truth. But you don't have to contaminate the truth with excessive thinking about your condition. If you do, you will only fill your remaining days with additional pain and suffering. The *now* is all anyone really has.

The quality of your life is determined solely by the relationship you have to your own thinking. If you find yourself anticipating death or thinking about illness, know that you do have another option. You can dismiss the thoughts that enter your mind the way you would shoo flies away from your picnic lunch. You can learn to live, really live, in the present moment.

Don't Attach Conditions to Your Contentment

If you are facing a serious or terminal illness, you don't have the luxury of time. Don't make the mistake of attaching unlikely conditions to your happiness, such as, 'I can only be happy if my illness disappears.' Happiness cannot occur when we place its source outside ourselves. If we assume that certain conditions must be met before we can feel contentment, we are too late to experience it. Many terminally ill patients report that they do experience fleeting moments of happiness or contentment, yet it's easy to let this good feeling pass you by without due notice. It's tempting to let your moments of happiness drift away with your next negative or fearful thought. You don't have to do this. You can stay in a good state of mind by remembering that your thoughts are the vehicle that rob you of your happiness.

It's OK to feel good even if your circumstances don't seem to warrant this more positive outlook. Fearful thoughts *will* continue to enter your mind but that doesn't mean you have to focus on them. If you think back, you will remember that fearful thoughts filled your head even when your body was healthy.

Healthy Psychological Functioning and Illness

Inner turmoil will *always* come about — whether or not you are physically ill — when you take the things you think about too seriously and blow them up in your mind as if they had a life of their own. For example, suppose that you are ill. Your doctor walks into the room and reports that you have taken a turn for the worse. Obviously this is regrettable news, but the truth is, you have two options. The first option involves healthy psychological functioning and consists of taking this information in one ear, letting it flow through your mind and out of the other ear. Doing so will keep your mind free enough to know what to do next. Should I relax more? Should I get another opinion? Should I take another course of action? Or should I simply accept my predicament and live each day to its fullest? Whatever your response, remaining in healthy functioning will allow you to take a course of ation or none at all. Whatever you decide to do, you won't allow your mind to become panicked or overly frustrated with self-pitying thoughts. Healthy functioning will allow you to see with the clearest possible head the best solution given the facts. Tapping into healthy functioning will also allow you to remain in the present moment enough to appreciate fully the gift of your life. Rather than focusing on what is yet to be, you will be able to remain calm. Healthy functioning allows you to live each moment that you have with gratitude and grace.

The second option involves unhealthy psychological functioning and also consists of taking in the information the doctor is delivering. But instead of letting it flow through your mind, you would have a 'thought attack' — focusing on and analysing the news to the point of becoming emotionally paralysed. So rather than using your available energy to live, you consume yourself with your own thoughts and come to the conclusion, 'Why me?' Instead of remaining in the present moment, you begin anticipating the worst. Rather than spending whatever remaining moments you have with as clear a mind as possible, allowing you to be with yourself or your family and loved ones, you allow your mind to race forward, consuming itself with fear.

Because unhealthy psychological functioning can turn even the smallest event into a personal nightmare in your mind, you can imagine how difficult it can be to handle something very traumatic, such as a serious or terminal illness. *It's critical to realize that tapping into your own healthy functioning is the best option you have.* It won't take away the illness but it will make you feel better about it.

Stress and Illness

In his book, *The Stress of Life,* Hans Selye demonstrates how adrenal exhaustion can be caused by severe emotional tension, such as great frustration or hopelessness. He goes on to detail many of the effects of negative emotions on body chemistry.

Just as clutching the steering-wheel and gritting our teeth doesn't make our car go any faster through traffic, thinking obsessively about an illness doesn't make it go away. In fact, it appears to be just the opposite. Emotional stress is very taxing on the body. It exhausts many of our vital healing mechanisms. I bring this to your attention to reiterate the practicality of what you are reading. Physical suffering is one of the most difficult issues a person will ever face. Unfortunately, without the understanding of how the mind can make matters even worse, the suffering you experience will increase.

The thoughts you have about your illness or death *are* going to enter your mind — and that's OK. It's up to you what you decide to do about them. Remembering that thoughts will always come and go is helpful. It gives you hope to know that there are many times when your mind is clear, when you are free to relax and enjoy your life. As you see how thoughts enter and leave your mind you are more able to contribute to this natural process. Rather than fighting your thoughts, wishing them away or pushing them away, you can begin to feel empowered by the knowledge that you are the one who is thinking them and that you can help yourself by letting them drift from your consciousness.

Perhaps the best way to summarize the importance of using your mind to your advantage is explained in Norman Cousins' classic book, *Anatomy of an Illness.* He describes how a 90-year-old man was able to use his mind to help his body.

Marta, having been through these reluctances before, reassured Don Pablo, saying she was certain he would be stimulated by the meeting. She reminded him that he liked the young people who did the last filming and that they would probably be back again. In particular, she called his attention to the lovely young lady who directed the recording.

Don Pablo brightened. 'Yes, of course,' he said, 'it will be good to see them again.'

As before, he stretched his arms in front of him and extended his fingers. Then the spine straightened and he stood up and went to his cello. He began to play. His fingers, hands, and arms were in sublime coordination as they responded to the demands of his brain for the controlled beauty of movement and tone. Any cellist thirty years his junior would have been proud to have such extraordinary physical command.

Twice in one day I have seen the miracle. A man almost ninety, beset with the infirmities of old age, was able to cast off his afflictions, at least temporarily, because he knew he had something of overriding importance to do. There was no mystery about the way it worked, for it happened every day. Creativity for Pablo Casals was the source of his own cortisone. It is doubtful whether any anti-inflammatory medication he would have taken would have been as powerful or as safe as the substances produced by the interaction of his body and mind.

He went on to say something that speaks to the essence of this chapter.

The process is not strange. If he had been caught up in an emotional storm, the effects would have been manifested in an increased flow of hydrochloric acid to the stomach, in an upsurge of adrenal activity, in the production of corticoids, in the increase of blood pressure, and a faster heart beat.

Not getting caught up in your own thoughts starts with the *intention* of not doing so. Thinking is a voluntary function, and each of us has the ability to dismiss thoughts that are bound to lead to 'an emotional storm'. Life can be so beautiful when we are not caught up in the coils of our own thoughts. Clearing the mind is the first step in appreciating this beauty.

16

Many Problems, One Solution

In the last two chapters we have covered some of the more difficult areas of life that, at some point, every one of us will have to deal with: grief, loss, pain, illness, and death. Needless to say, in addition to the areas we have discussed, there are many other significant problems in life that need to be coped with: communication between people, behaviours we have to change, financial concerns, dealing with difficult people, job and career concerns, raising children, and ageing, to name just a few.

My hope is that as you have been reading, you have begun to sense that in a very meaningful way *all* problems, regardless of their specific nature, have threads of consistency running through them. Every problem is made worse by what I refer to as 'analysis paralysis'. This is a situation in which a person wishing to solve a problem uses repeated and intense deliberation in the hope of coming up with a viable solution. This is where you try to figure out, make sense of, and most specifically, analyse your problems. The major problem with analysis, however, is that as you think excessively about a problem, your problem-orientated thoughts will begin to lower your spirits. And, as we have seen, if there is one certainty in life it is this: *when your spirits are low, your wisdom and common sense fly out of the window.* You simply aren't at your best and you don't see life clearly when you are feeling low. Since your feelings follow your thoughts, the more attention and emphasis you put on a problem, the worse you will feel and the less wisdom you will have access to.

Einstein once said, 'The solution to a problem will never come about from the same level of understanding that created the problem in the first place.' In other words, dwelling on problems will not help us overcome them, because we will be unable to see the answer we need. Solutions are found, on the other hand, when we see things in a new and fresh way, when we allow the wisdom that comes from a quiet mind (healthy functioning) to take over. As ironic and simplistic as it may seem, you need to stop thinking about a problem in order to see a new solution. As your mind clears of your concerns, answers will occur to you that were covered up by your thoughts of the problem. Wisdom is nothing more than seeing the same old problems in a new and fresh way.

All thoughts grow with attention, and problems are no exception to this rule. In a very real sense, dealing head on with a specific problem by focusing on it can be a tremendous mistake. The more we focus on a problem, whether it be related to finances, our children, other relationships, or a dying loved one, the less able we are to see a solution. This is why when someone repeatedly discusses your problems with you, you never seem to get anywhere. You go over the same sets of facts and come to the same conclusions. The only certainty in this dynamic is the way you will feel: frustrated, confused, and unhappy.

Perhaps you feel that the most basic problem you deal with is the fact that emotionally you don't feel very good. If this is the case, the same rule applies. Every time a thought enters your mind about how bad you feel, you have a choice. Do you think about it some more in the hope that keeping those thoughts alive in your head will somehow help you? Or do you dismiss the thought as simply another passing thought? In choosing this second option, you open the door to your healthy functioning. Chances are, a minute later (or even a few seconds later) another thought may enter your head about how bad you feel, or how bad you usually feel. If so, you can dismiss it as well. Each time you do so, you are getting used to paying less attention to the problem and more to feeling good.

It's true that habits of thinking are difficult to break, but they *can* be broken. One of the most significant findings in the field of psychology in recent years has been that we *can* choose the way we think. We are in charge — thinking is a voluntary function. Only habit makes us focus on the thoughts that enter our minds. It can also become a habit to dismiss the thoughts you have as they enter your mind.

If you look at the details of every problem that occurs in your life and try to make sense out of each one individually, then much of your life is going to be spent focused on your problems. You may indeed have some successes, yet the way you feel in general, won't change. When the car breaks down, you'll spend energy not only fixing the car but also thinking about it afterwards. The same will be true when you have a run-in with your boss or your spouse, when someone forgets to return your call, when something gets lost in the mail, as well as every other daily annoyance that comes up.

It may be true that you will never be completely free from life's little annoyances, but you can become free from *feeling* annoyed. The solution is to see that all of life's problems, big and small, are made worse by the fact that we think about them well after they are over or anticipate them well before we are confronted by them.

As you intentionally take your mind off your problems when they enter your mind, you will gradually begin to feel better, and as you feel better you are more equipped to solve your problems. Keep this in mind: *if you can't solve a problem in a positive state of mind, you will never be able to solve that problem in a lower state of mind.* Excessive thought about your problems won't help. When you understand that mental review works only to a very limited extent — and that 'analysis paralysis' is to be avoided at all costs — your inner wisdom will begin to take over.

Problems we encounter are always mood-related. When you are in a low mood, you will see slight annoyances as major obstacles, you will hear small suggestions as major criticisms, and you will think of future obstacles as being insurmountable. When your mood is low, any factor — personal or external — will seem to inhibit your experience and cause you unhappiness. In higher moods, you look beyond your circumstances, and simply do the best you can with who you are and what you have.

Life looks drastically different depending on how we are feeling. This is important to know because in higher feeling states, we already have what we want — to feel good. Our view of our problems will always change depending on our mood level. The higher our mood, the better our sense of perspective. It's senseless to think that solving any particular problem will create inner peace and make you happy — it won't. The next time you are feeling low, you'll see some other aspect of your life in an equally hopeless way. This is the nature of negative feeling states. The worse you feel, the more formidable your problems will seem.

I'm not suggesting that you shrug off your problems simply because you are in a low mood. But you will gain perspective on all problems, regardless of their specificity or magnitude, if you wait until you are in a higher mood.

This knowledge can shield you, to a large extent, from being devastated by the painful aspects you will face in your life. If you're grounded in the truth that life truly will look better soon, you can begin to move back to the original premise of this book, which is that *your thinking is responsible for your unhappiness*. You may not always be able to change your circumstances, but you always have at least some control over your own thinking.

17

Unhappiness is Your Curriculum

Everyone has issues, or a series of issues, that are central to this life, lessons that must be learned in order to arrive at a sense of inner peace. You can think of your central issue or issues as your 'curriculum', an education that you must go through to make your life feel complete. For some people, the central lesson in their life is physical — learning to live with diabetes or blindness, for example. Some people have a more emotional handicap, such as a strong resistance to intimacy, or untamed anger. The central issue in others' lives may take the form of an addiction to cigarettes, alcohol, drugs, food, and so forth.

When you study people and their issues, one theme becomes perfectly clear: the name of the game is learning how to deal effectively with, and eventually conquer, the central issues in your life. Sometimes conquering your curriculum means making the symptom go away. A person can learn, for example, to be intimate, even though it seemed impossible before she undertook the effort. At other times, conquering means coming to terms with a circumstance that can't be changed, such as a physical disability.

Everyone has a curriculum. Whatever curriculum a person is experiencing, be it physical, emotional, spiritual, or intellectual, it will initially be experienced as 'difficult' by that person, regardless of how others see it — if they see it as easy, it's because it's not their curriculum.

Every person has a curriculum and every curriculum can be overcome and conquered. Survivors of the Holocaust will testify to this truth. Despite the unspeakable conditions, there were many who survived, who learned to live, and even to forgive. And for each brave soul who did survive physically, there were undoubtedly hundreds or thousands of others who, despite their horrible circumstances, learned to live at peace before they were killed.

I'm not trying to evaluate the severity of any single curriculum, because each person's curriculum will be severe for them. What I am trying to do is to show you that every curriculum does indeed have a solution. Once you see that this is true, life becomes a game — and winning the game means enjoying your life. This is not intended to minimize the severity of your depression. I'm calling life a game because it is full of challenges, and challenges can be met.

Your curriculum is depression. What, then, is your strategy?

When you understand where your depression is coming from, and when you view it from a distance, the 'game' begins to change. Depression is no longer an emergency, something that is destroying your life, but rather a part of your 'course work', a necessary part of your education in life, something that you must learn to conquer. You can conquer it.

When you redefine your depression in this broader more educational sense, your depression takes on a more impersonal nature. By impersonal I mean you see it as being less about you and more about learning. When the feeling of depression comes up with this more impersonal perspective, you don't feel helpless — 'Oh no' — you feel challenged — 'Here I go again'. When you learn how to challenge your depression, depression as you know it will eventually cease to exist. There won't be any reason for depression to remain in your life because you will have learned your lesson. You will have gone through the process of conquering your depression. Now it will be time for a new curriculum to emerge in your life, new opportunities to learn. The game will change, and it will be better.

Seek Out Your Emotional Health

If you experience even the slightest relief, if you feel even one per cent better as you clear your mind and distrust what you think when you are low, then you are on your way! It means you have tapped into your healthy functioning, that part of you that is free of depression. Your job now is to nourish that part of yourself by knowing that it exists, respecting it, and wanting it more than anything else in your life. *You must want your emotional health even more than you want to get rid of your emotional distress.* Remember, your attention is the key to your success. If your attention is on how much you want to get rid of your pain, then your attention is on your pain. But if your attention is directed towards your healthy functioning, your inner peace, that is exactly where you will be headed.

Regardless of the issue you are dealing with, choosing your healthy functioning over your habitual response is going to be difficult. It will always be tempting to rationalize to yourself why your situation is unique, why it's more difficult for you, why it's appropriate or important to feel bad, why this time is too difficult to choose happiness. While every curriculum is unique, every solution is identical.

If my curriculum, for example, centres around an inability to handle criticism, if I shiver with rage at the slightest suggestion offered to me, there is only one solution — to use criticism as a vehicle towards greater inner strength. When a suggestion is offered, and I feel the struggle emerging within me, I must acknowledge the struggle yet choose my healthy functioning instead of my destructive urge. I must remind myself that I have a choice. I must have faith that my inner strength is more powerful than my helpless feeling of struggle. Each time I choose peace instead of fear, love instead of hate, happiness instead of struggle, I solidify my faith in my healthy functioning, and it gets easier.

Each step you take towards overcoming your curriculum brings you that much closer to a genuinely happy and contented life. Each time you consciously choose your healthy functioning over your thought system you are solidifying and strengthening your authentic inner power.

18

The Art of Optimism

When we are faced with any type of adversity, we naturally react by thinking about it. Most of us, however, forget, that we are the one who is doing the thinking, that we are actively manufacturing the thoughts we think. Our thoughts become so habitual to us that we don't even realize we are having them! Instead, we develop patterns of negative thought as our normal reaction to events and our way of coping with life, and believe that our life and our circumstances are responsible for the thoughts we are having. This isn't true! Since *we* are the ones doing the thinking, *we* are also the ones responsible for changing our thinking. When we realize this, we can shift from a pessimistic to a more optimistic outlook. You can learn to stop *all* negative trains of thought from developing before they have a chance to develop fully by taking responsibility for the fact that you are the driver of the train!

Suppose you have been working hard making a sweater for your daughter. While carrying the sweater to the car, you close the car door on it and it rips. If you are a pessimist, you may think to yourself, 'Nice going, idiot. Every time I try to do something, I screw it up.'

Unfortunately, this negative type of thinking won't be limited to the episode of tearing the sweater. If you are someone who is hard on yourself for innocent accidents such as this, chances are you will be hard on yourself most of the time. Whenever something painful or difficult happens to you, irrespective of how minor it may be — a sore throat, a memo from your employer, or an unreturned phone call — you imagine the absolute worst: a terrible flu coming on, losing your job, or your friend no longer likes you. The problem with pessimistic thinking, as you know by now, is that *your thoughts determine the way you feel.* In the example above, your thoughts would make you feel like an idiot, the sweater and your inability not to tear it having nothing to do with it. Because your thoughts determine the way you feel, negative thinking can be seen as an attempt to convince yourself that feeling bad is a good idea!

Pessimistic thinking leads to feeling sorry for yourself, unhappiness, even depression — which further leads to an overall pessimistic outlook on life. Negative thinking can creep insidiously into your mind and fuel the compelling urge to pay attention to that negative thinking. In a strange way, it's tempting to believe that you are going to somehow feel better if you continue to think in this way — if you just think it through enough. Unfortunately, feeling better isn't the result of thinking negatively. The more you pay attention to and go along with your negative thoughts, the worse you will feel — every single time. This is a critical point that so many of us forget: *negative thinking gets us nowhere, except perhaps a one-way ticket to the emotional doldrums!*

The way you feel about yourself and about life would be so much nicer if, when ripping the sweater, you thought to yourself, 'Hey, it's all right. Accidents happen to everyone. Don't worry about it. I'll fix it the best I can.' This simple change of attitude amounts to nothing more than changing your habitual responses. The shift is small but the dividends are great. Learning to think more positively will affect the way you feel. It's the single most important decision you can make in the development of mental health.

You may be used to thinking about things in a certain way, yet you are fully capable of changing the way you look at life once you make the commitment to do so. Starting today, change the way you think, especially during difficult times, and the quality of your life will rise dramatically.

But how do you make the transition? Making an internal shift from negativity to a more positive outlook is easier than you might think. The shift involves three simple steps: (1) the recognition and admission that you are in the habit of thinking negatively; (2) the understanding that your thoughts originate within yourself, that it's something you are actively doing to create your psychological experience of life; and (3) seeing the innocence of negative thinking. Let's take a brief look at these three steps.

The habit of negative thinking

If you are in the habit of thinking in negative terms, you are going to be tempted to dismiss this information as too simplistic to be effective. A pessimist would tend to think this way — you wouldn't expect a pessimist to think that there was the possibility for change.

You must realize that negativity is just a habit that, unfortunately, has been reinforced many thousands of times. A negative attitude, however, isn't carved in stone, it's not wired into your consciousness the same way the colour of your eyes is genetically determined for life. Negativity is a learned response to the events of your life. There are millions who have learned to look at life more optimistically, and you can be one of them.

Your thoughts originate within you

The idea that your thoughts originate within yourself

is a central theme of this book. You are the manufacturer of the thoughts that run through your head. The real power in your life is with you, the producer of your thoughts, not the thoughts themselves. If you don't have a clear understanding that you are the thinker, it's unrealistic to believe that you can change your attitude. Without this healthy knowledge as a foundation, it's too easy to be seduced by your own thoughts. As something happens in your life that you wish hadn't happened, a thought will enter your mind, such as 'Nothing ever goes smoothly.' As it does, you will feel justified in feeling sorry for yourself, which will lead in turn to more negative thoughts. Once you are grounded in the idea that you are the one who just had that thought, however, and that your thoughts aren't just something that happened to you, you open the door to new options. Remember, you manufactured them! Now when a negative thought enters your mind you can say to yourself, 'Here I go again. I'm not going to fall into this trap anymore. Of course things go smoothly for me some of the time.'

Seeing the innocence

Everyone has certain habits they would like to eliminate. If you look at habits, most of them began innocently enough. Very few people set out to become drug addicts, alcoholics, lifelong smokers, or even nail-biters. Instead, most habits are developed slowly over time by becoming comfortable and familiar through repetition. For example, a drinker learns to reach for a drink whenever he feels stressed. Even though the alcohol makes matters worse, the alcohol and its effects are familiar. The drinker doesn't know what else to do.

Negative thinkers are in a similar boat. Something happens and thoughts enter the mind as a learned response. No one actually wants to have thoughts like,

'Life isn't worth living,' or 'I'm not happy.' Rather, these
and other negative thoughts are drummed up just
because they are familiar. They seem to just appear in
the mind — and because they do, many negative thinkers
believe they do so for a reason. In other words, there
must be some justification for the thoughts they are
having. A negative thinker will always be able to point
to reasons why he feels negative — his car isn't working,
no one wants to talk to him, no one appreciates him,
and so on. Negative thinking always seems justified.

Although it seems justified, it's important to realize
that *the events that you think are causing you to think
negatively aren't the problem.* I can assure you that anyone
can learn to deal with a person who doesn't appreciate
them or a car that isn't working well. No one, however,
can withstand the negative influence of self-defeating,
negative thinking for too long. Eventually, everyone
must either learn to think more positively or face
ongoing unhappiness and depression.

Negative thinking was learned innocently. You didn't
set out to hurt yourself. You can learn to forgive
yourself and give yourself a second chance at life when
you see how easy it was to fall into the trap. It's true
that some people seem to be natural optimists, but many
of us had to learn how to be optimists. We had to change
the way we think in order to feel better.

It's important to know the powerful role that your
beliefs play in creating your life experience and the way
you feel. If you think of yourself, 'I'm always being
ripped off,' it's not a coincidence that you feel like a
victim. If you think, 'If people only knew how difficult
my life is,' it's not a coincidence that you feel burdened.
Circumstances don't make a person, they reveal
him! Your life doesn't make you feel bad, your thinking
does.

Your attitude towards life and your beliefs about life originate within you. The way you look at life isn't something that happens to you — it's something that you make up, moment by moment, as you move through life. At any moment in your life you can decide to change your attitude. Your attitude is made up of one thing and one thing only — your own thoughts. Change them, and your world will change.

Habits are often very hard to break. This is especially true, as we discussed in chapter 9, when dealing with the habit of negative thinking. You are accustomed to thinking about things in a certain way. You may have reinforced your negative thinking thousands of times throughout your lifetime. Each negative reinforcement convinced you further that you were essentially right: life isn't all that good.

Try to imagine how much better your life would seem if you had a more positive outlook. What would it be like if, in response to an unfortunate event, you thought to yourself, 'I'm glad it wasn't worse'? What would happen to your negative feelings if you no longer thought negative thoughts?

What is it that prevents you from thinking more positively? The answer is stubbornness. Unless you don't accept the fact that your thoughts determine the way you feel, stubbornness is your only true obstacle. There is some way that you are deciding that negative thinking is more important to you than feeling good. It has been my experience that anyone can learn the art of optimism.

Rachel was one of the most negative people I have ever met. To her, life was miserable. She was unhappy, even depressed much of the time, but couldn't think of any specific reasons for her unhappiness. She just felt bad.

Therapists and friends advised Rachel to 'change her

life'. It was suggested that she get involved in the community, meet new people, change her job, move to a new apartment, and so forth. She made all these changes, and more, yet she was still miserable. Why?

Here is a typical conversation I had with Rachel when I first met her:

Therapist: 'How's work going?'
Rachel: 'Okay, but kind of slow. I hope the economy doesn't scare away all the customers.'
Therapist: 'Rachel, I understand you are getting involved in some charitable work.'
Rachel: 'Yeah, but it's kind of discouraging, so many people are hurting.'
Therapist: 'Is your new boyfriend interested in the agency you are volunteering for?'
Rachel: 'He is, but I think he's only getting involved in my behalf.'

It didn't take long to discover why Rachel was so unhappy. If you look at her answers to my questions, you will see that every single reply contained a negative element. She was a pessimist in every sense of the word. Seeing the negative, or potential negative, in a given situation was her way of relating to life. It was absurd to think that changing her circumstances was going to help her. When I met her, Rachel would have been disappointed at winning the pools! Interestingly, when I first mentioned the word 'pessimistic', Rachel didn't think it applied to her. She felt she was a 'realist'.

Rachel's turnaround came as she began to see that virtually everything she thought about had a negative tone to it. It was a habit for Rachel to look at life negatively. Negative thoughts would enter her mind and she would react to them as if it were her obligation to do so.

It wasn't easy for Rachel to see that her thoughts about life were just thoughts. She felt her thoughts had a great deal of merit. She didn't think of herself as negative, but that as a realist it was always important to her to point out the facts. Of course the way she looked at the facts always reinforced her positions. Rachel felt that her attitude was justified. After all, she insisted, 'things can go wrong and it's important to be prepared.'

Rachel learned that it's *impossible* for anyone to feel good when they fill their head with negativity. She learned one of the most important principles in this book: *you feel the way you do because of the thoughts you are having.* When I reminded her that her single goal in coming to see me was to feel better, she began to see that to achieve her goal, she *must* begin to eliminate her negative thoughts. Further, Rachel had to realize that her responses to life were not carved in stone — they were simply a habit that was keeping her miserable. She was on an emotional merry-go-round with her own thinking. First she would think negatively, then she would feel bad. Her bad feelings would then encourage her to think more negatively — and so she would. And on and on and on.

Fortunately, this merry-go-round can move in two directions. As Rachel began dismissing her habitual, negative thinking, she began to feel better. And as she felt better, fewer and fewer negative thoughts entered her mind, which made her feel increasingly optimistic about life.

Rachel is not unique. Anyone can learn the art of optimism, but it does take humility and courage. You must have the humility to admit that your thinking *is* negative and you must have the courage to set about changing it. If you set your mind to it, you can learn the art of optimism, one of the most important steps in developing a life filled with happiness and gratitude.

19

Happiness and Gratitude

If you have some vague or incomplete idea of what happiness is, you are very likely to miss it when it arrives. It will pass you by because you won't know what you're looking for, even if it's right there in front of you — which it is. But if you do understand what happiness is, and where it comes from, you will recognize and appreciate it when it does surface, thus avoiding the common tendency to let it drift away with your thoughts.

Happiness

There is no 'way to happiness'. Happiness *is* the way. Happiness is a feeling that you tap into, not an outcome of events. When you understand this important distinction you will, at the very least, be looking in the right direction. You will be able to encourage the feeling of happiness to surface, and stay with the feeling when it arrives, rather than letting it go and continuing to look elsewhere for its source. Each time you start looking for happiness outside yourself, and each time you try to think your way to happiness, it will slip through your fingers because your mind will have drifted away from its source.

When you find yourself saying something like, 'I'll be happy someday,' or 'I hope to be happy someday,' what you are *really* saying is, 'Someday I hope to be able to take my attention *off* my problems, concerns, and negativity, and put it *on* a nicer feeling, the feeling of love.' Most people, however, are not going to wake up one day and suddenly find themselves ignoring their bad feelings and basking in their positive feelings. It's going to take practice. Whether you start today, or 10 years from now, you are simply going to have to stop postponing what it takes to be happy. Sooner or later you will have to take that leap of faith and say to yourself, 'OK, my life may not be perfect, but there is never going to be a better time for me to put my attention where it needs to be — on that nicer feeling inside myself that lies beneath my negative thoughts.' Why not start right now, today, this very moment? This is a very important question to ask yourself, one that must be answered correctly if you wish to be on your way to happiness.

Once you start to see the relationship between your thinking and the way that you feel — the immediate relationship and the cumulative relationship — you are on your way to a life with less depression. Waiting until next year doesn't help. After all, what are you waiting for? The conditions for a new life will never be better. Now is the time. You are still going to have to implement your new understanding, and you are still going to have to practise what you have learned. And even though you have a new understanding about yourself that can help you, it will still be true that when you fall back into your old habits and follow negative trains of thought, or when you accumulate negative mental baggage, it's going to harm and upset you, and you will still have to redirect your thinking and your attention.

When you spend time around happy people, one of the first things you notice about them is that they are not always happy. They are generally happy, meaning their overall feeling about life is extremely positive, but they, too, have their own share of emotional ups and downs. Remember, everyone has moods, including very low moods, and in those low moods life will seem really bad. And everyone, too, will have negativity stream through their minds from time to time. Happy people, however, actually notice the negativity forming in their minds more often than those who consider themselves unhappy. This makes sense, because their noticing negativity followed by their dropping negativity is the very act which keeps them happy. They will actually have many of the same thoughts as unhappy people, but their relationship to those thoughts will be completely different. Happy people will see their thoughts as thoughts. They will strive to ignore and drop as many negative thoughts as they can. They will look for a feeling of happiness even when their circumstances don't seem to warrant a positive outlook. They are not pretending to be happy, they are looking to be happy. They know that what they are looking for is a happy feeling, not a perfect life. Happiness comes first, and a good life comes out of feeling happy. When they do find themselves being pulled towards negativity or when they get caught up in 'analysis paralysis', they know they have to change what they are doing, and fast, if they want to get back on track towards happiness.

Unhappy people have a different type of relationship to their thinking from happy people. When unhappy people have a negative thought or series of thoughts, they tend to follow them out of habit or to see whether or not doing so will make them feel better. It will not! Unhappy people don't see their thoughts as thoughts, they see them as reality, as important. They rarely ignore the thoughts that bring them down, but instead analyse or study them, thus giving them additional life, and making them seem even more formidable and important than they really are. One of the greatest distinctions I have seen between happy people and unhappy people is the willingness to admit that their thinking is dysfunctional. Happy people jump at the opportunity to admit that their thinking is the cause of their unhappiness. They admit it. They want to eliminate, as much as possible, the thoughts that are interfering with their joy. They are delighted that it's them, and not someone else, that is responsible for their happiness. Unhappy people are usually far less willing, or able, to admit that their head is full of negativity. They will insist, 'I don't have very many negative thoughts. I don't think negatively, I just feel depressed.' This is the most painful denial you can ever experience, because it wrongly suggests that you are not in control of your own life — although you can be.

The act of admitting that it's *you* creating depression for yourself through your own thinking is a very empowering and healing admission. Once you do, you then have some control over the direction and action you will take. Prior to admitting that your thinking is causing your suffering, it's very easy to feel like a victim if you believe that your depression is something that is happening *to* you rather than something you are doing to yourself?

Happiness is a feeling, nothing more, and nothing less. It's not complicated and it's not hard to obtain. Happiness doesn't require a perfect life to manifest itself, and it certainly doesn't come about through years of analysis. If you want to be happy, study happy people. The happiest lives are not the most analysed. In fact, it has been my experience that the happiest lives are often the simplest lives — externally, and especially internally. Happy people are too busy being happy and enjoying their lives to study their unhappiness. True, they feel unhappy from time to time, everyone does, but why study it? Acknowledging it and allowing it to pass away is all you really have to do.

When you understand the tickings of your own psychological clock — how your thinking affects the way you feel, how your low moods can make your life seem far worse than it really is, and the difference between your natural state of mind and your analytical mind — you can access that place inside yourself where depression can never exist. You have it in you to tap into a nicer feeling. Be happy and treasure your life.

Gratitude

Gratitude is the antidote for depression. It's a very powerful feeling that stems, like all feelings, from your thinking.

But how do you feel grateful if you have been depressed? What would you say if I offered you £1000 for everything you could think of to feel grateful for? You'd probably say, 'How much time do I have?' You would think of hundreds of things to be grateful for because you would be thinking purposefully. If your internal antenna is looking for gratitude, it will find it! As I have discussed, however, habits are hard to break, especially habits having to do with your own thinking. If you are in the habit of seeing the glass half empty instead of half full, you are going to have to challenge that habit if you want to live your life with a sense of gratitude.

How do you go about feeling grateful? The process itself is quite simple: (1) your intention must be to feel grateful — you have to want it. You must understand what's in it for you, and what's in it for everyone else; (2) you have to remember that gratitude is the very essence of your healthy psychological functioning. It's your most natural state of mind. Because of this, in the absence of negative thoughts, you are left with a feeling of gratitude. Because gratitude is natural, you have had to learn *not* to feel gratitude; and (3) you have to admit that your negativity is a habit. You are the thinker of your own thoughts and it's only your thinking that is holding your negativity in place. You have it in you to change your entire attitude today! You are the boss and you are in control of your thinking by making the commitment to change it. As you dismiss the negative thoughts that interfere with your feeling of happiness you will discover more gratitude surfacing in your life.

But why do you even want to feel gratitude? Very simply, because gratitude feels good and it brings out the best in you. Everything in this book points to gratitude. It's the epitome of healthy functioning in action. When you feel grateful, everything in your life looks good, and you feel good. Once you recognize gratitude as a force in your life, it will begin to permeate your entire existence. The beneficiaries of this grateful feeling will be your self-esteem, your relationships, your well-being, your career, your hopes, your dreams, your problems, your unborn discoveries and your future. When you live in a feeling of gratitude, the rest of your life will take care of itself. If you can't solve a problem when you are feeling gratitude, then more than likely that problem can't be solved!

As you have seen, the relationship you have to your own thinking is the most significant factor in determining the quality of your life. This is because your thinking directs the way you feel. The feeling you live in depends entirely on where your focus of attention lies. If you learn to focus on and feel grateful for what you have in each moment, that thought process will become a habit itself. Similarly, when you focus on what is lacking in or wrong with your life, you will always find a way to attract even more of what you don't like.

Starting right now, you, too, can be happy. Begin looking for what's right in your life. Keep looking and don't give up until seeing what's right becomes a habit. Practise feeling grateful even if you don't feel like it because very soon you will find yourself enjoying yourself as you never have before.

One of the most common questions I am asked is, 'If I walked around feeling grateful all the time, wouldn't I turn into a selfish person?' The answer to this question is a certain *no!* What do you really offer other people? You offer them your presence, your well-being, yourself. When you feel good, others around you will feel good. When you feel fulfilled, your good feelings spread to the rest of the world. On the other hand, when you feel down, you are so consumed with your own negativity that you can't possibly have anything left for anyone else. What can you offer someone else if you can't even take care of yourself? So feeling gratitude is both selfish and selfless. You win and everyone else wins.

Finally, and most important, the greatest power you have to deepen the feeling of gratitude in your life is to notice the feeling *when it is there.* Never force the feeling, but when it's there, take notice. Remember, it's your attention that makes any feeling grow. Don't let even small feelings of gratitude drift away with your thoughts. Instead, notice how they feel and help them grow. The warmth and comfort of that feeling as it grows is one of the nicest feelings you can experience as a human being.

It's interesting to discover that you don't need to have anything in particular to be grateful for in order to feel gratitude. Instead, all you have to do is want to feel it. Again, this is due to the fact that gratitude stems from your thinking and not from the circumstances in your life. Gratitude is an attitude towards life that has nothing whatsoever to do with what you have or don't have. This is why you will often meet people who on the surface have little to be grateful for, but who feel a genuine sense of deep gratitude for the gift of life. These people aren't fooling themselves with their gratitude — they simply have a positive attitude. They look at what they have while most others focus on what they don't have.

Luckily, you can always take the path of healthy functioning, the path of gratitude. Instead of following your negative trains of thought, disconnect from them. Remember happiness and gratitude, which are the feelings you have been looking for, the answer you need. They are more powerful than depression. Try these new feelings today and watch your entire experience as a human being change before your eyes. You have it in you to change today, right now. A change of heart can happen in an instant, in this moment.

How to Feel Good Again

You feel good again by understanding that depression is something that forms within your own thinking. As I've mentioned before, your thinking is not the same as reality. You produce real thoughts, but that is all they are. You don't have to be frightened by your own thinking once you understand that your thinking is *not* something that is happening to you, but something that *you* are doing to create your experience. You don't need to produce thoughts and then be depressed by those thoughts. Thoughts come and they go. Like a river carrying leaves, your mind produces a never-ending supply of thoughts. Some are nice, some are not, but all of them are just thoughts. You are free to reach out and grab any thought you wish, but keep in mind that you are the one doing the reaching and the grabbing. If you can remember that it's you doing the thinking, you will create the necessary distance and perspective between yourself and your thinking, thus protecting yourself against the negative effects of thought.

You feel good again when you stop believing that you are thinking when you are down. Everyone feels low at least some of the time. When you are feeling low you will always feel an urgent need to figure out why you feel the way you do. You must resist this urge. You don't have to figure out anything. The only thoughts you will be able to manufacture when you are low are negative thoughts, so all your thinking will be counter-productive. You must wait for and look for the part of you that isn't depressed before you try to figure anything out. Once you feel better, your healthy func-tioning will do all the figuring for you, answers will seem obvious, and you will have a better perspective, wisdom, and common sense.

You feel good again when you understand that depression is nothing more than an extended, very low mood. When you stop participating in the destructive tendencies (thinking, analysing, figuring, worrying, talking) that seem appropriate when you are low, and you instead turn your attention towards your healthy functioning, a nicer, more peaceful feeling will begin to emerge. It is then, when your perspective comes back, that you can resume your thinking, and get on with your life. The difference between a happy person and a depressed person isn't that the happy person never gets low — he does. But the happy person realizes that being low is as much a part of life as being high — she just doesn't believe what she thinks when she is low. She distrusts herself because she knows she is out of sorts. She hesitates before she thinks. She doesn't study her unhappiness — she looks for her happiness.

You feel good again when you realize that your

attention is the only glue holding your thinking in place. Without attention, your thinking disappears. When negative thoughts are filling your mind, your attention will help them grow even bigger. The more attention you give them, the bigger they get. But just because negative thoughts are in your mind doesn't mean you have to feed them. You can deflate your depression by putting your attention elsewhere: on your healthy functioning, on love and well-being. Your healthy functioning is all that's left when your attention is off your negativity. You can't miss it. It's the result of a clear mind, a mind that refuses to feed the negativity that enters it. Everyone has negativity enter his mind — and everyone can learn to turn it away. When you learn this skill you will have regained the power of your own life. You will no longer be a victim of your own thinking because you alone will decide which thoughts are worth focusing on and which ones are better left alone.

You feel good again when you understand that every moment in your life is a choice point. Negative thoughts may continue to enter your mind, and the most important question you must ask yourself is: 'What do I do when the negativity arrives?' Do you surrender and feed the negativity, or do you rise to the challenge? Can you let the negative thoughts go? Can you let them pass without feeding them? Can you give them the message that they are not important to you, that you want them to go away? Can you avoid the mistake of putting attention on your negativity in order to rid yourself of it? Can you direct your attention towards your healthy functioning even though it seems you don't have any? You have a choice. You are in charge of the direction you take when you are at this fork in the road. You can try to think your way out of your depression — which you won't be able to do — or you can look for and find your healthy functioning.

You feel good again when you start living in the present moment. The next time you feel depressed notice where your thoughts are. They will undoubtedly be somewhere else — either somewhere in the future or reviewing the past. But the future and the past are just thoughts, whereas life is right now. As you bring your attention inwards, closer to the now, and as you drop your thoughts relating to the future and the past, you will notice that your depressing thoughts will begin to disappear.

You feel good again when you see that life is like a pendulum. You are constantly swinging back and forth between your thought system and your healthy functioning. The fact that so many people don't recognize their healthy functioning doesn't mean that it doesn't exist. It does. It just seems so natural that it may pass unnoticed. It always exists when your mind is quiet and clear, when your thinking is not focused on your 'problems'.

If there were a single idea I could leave you with, it would be this: *live your life in the present moment and be grateful that you have that moment.* The present moment is where you will find your mental health and happiness. When you understand your own thinking enough not to let it sabotage your life, you will have the only tools you need to conquer your depression. Your life will be rich, satisfying and joyful. You *will* feel good again.

Index